Elmer Towns is a friend to pastors. His advice comes out of his own life—and he's never one to be afraid to teach from his scars. This book opened my eyes and heart to not only have a Sunday School, but to make it a high value!

DR. WAYNE CORDEIRO
NEW HOPE CHRISTIAN FELLOWSHIP

Dr. Stan Toler and Dr. Elmer Towns are men with a passion and concern for the Sunday School. Their books have inspired and informed workers around the country, and this new book is no exception. In it they give solid biblical and practical reasons why you should dedicate your energies and direct your attention to the work of the Sunday School. They also provide new and innovative ways to expand the effectiveness and increase the influence of your Sunday School. This book gives proven principles and fresh insight into how you can package your Sunday School for growth and reaching people for Jesus Christ.

DAVID W. GRAVES
DIRECTOR, SUNDAY SCHOOL MINISTRIES
INTERNATIONAL CHURCH OF THE NAZARENE

Elmer Towns and Stan Toler have done it again! These two servants of the church have reminded us of the greatest opportunity available to the church today, the Sunday School. There has never been a greater need than there is today for well-educated Christians in the marketplace. The Sunday School has not only survived the test of time but it is also once again thriving. Towns and Toler put this very practical, insightful and effective plan into our hands so that we can build a great Sunday School.

MARTY GRUBBS
SENIOR PASTOR, CROSSINGS COMMUNITY CHURCH
OKLAHOMA CITY, OKLAHOMA

What Every Pastor Should Know About Sunday School is an invaluable resource for pastors in revitalizing this essential ministry. Dr. Elmer Towns and Dr. Stan Toler share from their years of experience and deep commitment to the strategic importance of Sunday School. Their conversation with pastors emphasizes the priority of Sunday School in the church for all ages. I encourage each Pentecostal Holiness pastor to obtain this book.

BISHOP JAMES D. LEGGETT
GENERAL SUPERINTENDENT
INTERNATIONAL PENTECOSTAL HOLINESS CHURCH

Towns and Toler are worth the read. They offer a new paradigm for a tested tool. Their book will center your energies on the essentials of sound ministry. Theirs is a call to meaningful Bible teaching, warm fellowship, powerful prayer and strong character development through the simple structure of the Sunday School.

RALPH MOORE
PASTOR, HOPE CHAPEL, KANEOHE BAY, HAWAII
AUTHOR, *STARTING A NEW CHURCH*

I want every pastor in the Southern Baptist Convention to read this book because the foundation to revival in our churches is a strong Bible-teaching Sunday School. Also, the key to turning around the moral bankruptcy of our nation is instructing young people in the Word of God. Not only should every Southern Baptist pastor read this book, I would like every pastor in America to read it.

ADRIAN ROGERS
SENIOR PASTOR, BELLEVUE BAPTIST CHURCH
MEMPHIS, TENNESSEE

WHAT EVERY PASTOR

SHOULD KNOW ABOUT

SUNDAY SCHOOL

ELMER L. TOWNS
& STAN TOLER

Regal

From Gospel Light
Ventura, California, U.S.A.

Regal

PUBLISHED BY REGAL BOOKS
VENTURA, CALIFORNIA, U.S.A.
PRINTED IN THE U.S.A.

Regal Books is a ministry of Gospel Light, an evangelical
Christian publisher dedicated to serving the local church. We believe
God's vision for Gospel Light is to provide church leaders with
biblical, user-friendly materials that will help them evangelize,
disciple and minister to children, youth and families.

It is our prayer that this Regal book will help you discover
biblical truth for your own life and help you meet the needs
of others. May God richly bless you.

*For a free catalog of resources from Regal Books/Gospel Light, please call your
Christian supplier or contact us at* 1-800-4-GOSPEL *or*
www.regalbooks.com.

Rights for publishing this book in other languages are
contracted by Gospel Light Worldwide, the international nonprofit
ministry of Gospel Light. Gospel Light Worldwide also provides
publishing and technical assistance to international publishers
dedicated to producing Sunday School and Vacation Bible School
curricula and books in the languages of the world. For additional
information, visit www.gospellightworldwide.org; write to
Gospel Light Worldwide, P.O. Box 3875, Ventura, CA 93006; or send
an e-mail to info@gospellightworldwide.org.

Cover and interior design by Robert Williams
Edited by Rose Decaen

Library of Congress Cataloging-in-Publication Data
Towns, Elmer L.
  What every pastor should know about Sunday school / Elmer
Towns and Stan Toler.
      p.   cm.
Includes bibliographical references.
   ISBN 0-8307-2859-7
  1. Sunday schools.   I. Toler, Stan.   II. Title.
   BV1521.3 T69 2002
   268—dc21   2002013669

1 2 3 4 5 6 7 8 9 10 / 09 08 07 06 05 04 03 02

105155

DEDICATION

To Jack Hollingsworth

a Sunday School teacher who became Dad to me after my
father was killed in a tragic accident. Thanks for being a
faithful teacher of the Word, for marrying Mom, caring for
me and my two brothers and for seeing to it that I was the
first Toler to ever get a college education. I love you, Dad!

To Jimmy Breland

who picked up Elmer Towns in a Jewel Tea route truck,
took him faithfully to Sunday School, taught him the Bible
in the junior class and helped build character in his life.
Eastern Heights Presbyterian Church
Savannah, Georgia
1938-1990

CONTENTS

MAKING
YOUR CHURCH
HEALTHIER

Does your church need to grow healthier? How would you like to find a program that would help your church grow spiritually, numerically and financially? Put that checkbook away. It's not something you can buy. Chances are, you've already got it! We're talking about your Sunday School or small-group ministry. And we want to help equip you with a strategy to make your church healthier through building the Bible-teaching ministry of Sunday School.

The brainchild of Robert Raikes and D. L. Moody, Sunday School has served as both a spiritual incubator and launching pad for untold millions who have trusted Christ for the forgiveness of their past and a hope for their tomorrow.

This isn't a book about the *future* of Sunday School or small groups. This is a *present tense* reminder that in most cases the golden hour of church ministry is already on your calendar. Let's take that Bible teaching to a new level.

We're not asking you to neglect any other vital program in your Kingdom-building efforts, whether it happens on Sunday, Saturday or any other day of the week. These post-9/11 days demand our diligent and dedicated efforts to imitate one of the first superintendents of Bible teachers, the apostle Paul. He commanded teaching (see Rom. 12:7), mentoring (see 2 Tim. 2:2) and innovative ministry when he said, "I have become all things to all men, that I might by all means save some" (1 Cor. 9:22).

This book is about teaching . . . mentoring . . . and innovative ministry!

If Paul had had PowerPoint available in his day, you can be sure he would have run an extension cord from the kitchen out to the deck for that small-group Bible lesson presentation. He knew the value of packaging proven biblical principles with practical methods, presenting his package in an atmosphere of fellowship and discipling and marketing it to those searching for the truth.

This book may answer questions that aren't even being asked in some circles. But we're convinced that the larger circle of pastors and staff are looking for something to plug the holes in the member-leaking basements of their local churches. This book is about using Sunday School to keep people in your church and keep them growing in Christ.

The church and Sunday School doesn't have to be *us* against *them*. With some concentrated effort—and an old-fashioned revival of Bible teaching that really changes lives—your church can become more healthy. All that most people need is an invitation to join with a group of seekers to spend time discovering the Bible.

We want to challenge pastors not to overlook the benefits of one of the most proven fellowship-building . . .

disciple-blossoming . . .

answer-giving . . .

leader-equipping . . .

character-forming agencies already in your church: the Sunday School!

We're not preaching to the choir.

We've just pulled up a chair next to *your* desk—or that round table at the corner coffee shop—to have a chat with you about some imperative reasons why every pastor should sharpen the tool that is his Sunday School ministry. But we don't want you to keep this to yourself! Use this book to educate your staff or church board about the positive, life-giving effects of Sunday School.

And in case your laptop is booted up, the following pages will give you some things to save in one of those ministry "folders" under the filename "What I should know about Sunday School."

—Stan Toler and Elmer Towns

Chapter 1

SUNDAY SCHOOL
WILL HELP YOU
REACH THE LOST

Ron was hesitant to offer an invitation to salvation to his Sunday School class. After all, these were all good church people. His church was located in a rapidly growing suburb of Atlanta, so there were new attendees almost every week. But they all seemed to be "churched." Many of them even brought Bibles to class. *How can I offer the plan of salvation to* Christians? Ron wondered. *Won't it be insulting?*

But the lesson that day centered on Jesus' invitation to Nicodemus. "You must be born again" (John 3:7). So Ron decided to throw out an offer: "If you've never been born again by putting your faith in Jesus, you can be—right now."

To his surprise, several group members responded and prayed to receive the Lord that day.

"Nobody had ever told me that I needed to be saved," Jill, a middle-aged schoolteacher, said with astonishment.

Her husband had heard the phrase "born again," but he had never known what it meant. He said, "I've been going to church for almost five years, and I've never been invited to receive Jesus."

This couple is not alone. Thousands of unsaved people attend church every week. Attracted by uplifting worship services, vibrant family programs and good fellowship, many of their needs are met by the church, even though they are not believers. Sunday School—with its casual interaction and direct study of the Bible—is the place where they can be challenged spiritually. In a small-group interaction, they become personally involved with the Bible and God.

> ▶ *The platform attracts visitors, but small groups bond them to the church.*

The Reaching Arm

Historically, Sunday School has been called the *reaching* arm of the church. Contests, Sunday School buses, visitation programs and other techniques have pulled newcomers into the fellowship of the church. Through what was called *front-door evangelism* or *inviting evangelism*, many of those newcomers are now leaders in the church. Historically, visitors to the church came through the *Sunday School door*.

Today, most visitors to the church enter through the *worship door* instead of Sunday School. Many of these newcomers are often unsaved. In today's contemporary worship service, an unsaved person will feel the presence of God in the service. That's because when people worship God, He will come to "dwell within the praises of His people" (Ps. 22:3, author's translation). Remember, the Father seeks worshipers (see John 4:24).

The modern formula is that the platform attracts visitors, but small groups *bond them to the church*. This means visitors will attend your worship service, but you must get them into a small group, such as an adult Bible study, to help them become a part of the family life of the church.

For evangelistic outreach, well-planned and relevant worship services are a must. Flannel-board sermons and organ-solo specials won't hold the interest of our fast-paced, media-fed society. Pastors must include visual illustrations and timely topics. Musicians are well advised to offer the best-practiced and best-performed music possible. PowerPoint presentations for sermon outlines, Scripture reading, singing and lighting modules have found their rightful place in the sanctuary. But the Sunday School must assist this fast-paced evangelism in order for the church to be productive as a whole.

Action Point: How will Sunday School help preserve the evangelistic results of your worship service?

The Teaching Arm

The modern church must teach. Why? Because people do not know the Word of God; people do not know how to live for God; people are ignorant of spiritual things. One teenager thought Noah's ark was married to Joan of Ark, and the only reference to the Ten Commandments another teen could repeat was "Freedom of Speech." Yet another was asked, "Who was swallowed by the whale?" The answer was "Pinocchio."

Jesus commanded us "to make disciples in all ethnic groups . . . identify them in Christian fellowship with baptism . . . and teach them how to apply all truth taught by Him" (Matt. 28:19-20, author's translation). Notice the three parts of the Great Commission. First, evangelize by discipleship; second, build new believers up in the local body; third, teach individuals Bible truths and godly living.

Action Point: Will Sunday School fulfill your twenty-first century need to teach the Bible?

The Friendly Arm

If your church is oriented toward the twenty-first century, that's great! But remember, a high-tech church must lead to a "high-touch" ministry.

Time-weary citizens cross your church's threshold. Twenty-first-century living has become a maze of zeros and single digits. Binary code seems to be the DNA of our modern world. People need a friend, not just a friendly face. They need to feel someone is personally caring about the eternal condition of their soul.

As churches grow, so do the possibilities of impersonal ministry. As emphases change, there is a greater chance that the church and its ministry staff might lose their focus. Jesus reminded, "But seek first the kingdom of God and His righteousness, and all these things shall be added to you" (Matt. 6:33). Remember, the Kingdom comes first! The highest priority of the local church ministry is to get people into the Kingdom, not just into the church building.

The Sunday School has always been a wonderful place for newcomers to meet believers face-to-face. Its Bible-honoring, caring atmosphere is a home for seeking hearts. Its emphasis on the needs of the individual rather than the needs of the church is also a welcome relief. It is a safe place in which victims who are suffering from an impersonal society can be treated with love and compassion.

Action Point: Take time to visit various Sunday School classes and observe how visitors are included in the activities. Do we have a friendly Sunday School that starts with a friendly staff?

The Saving Arm

It's important to see the Sunday School as a tool for reaching the lost. While your Sunday School may not be the "first touch" for visitors, it may be the "final stop" that gets them to settle down in your church. So you must see the Sunday School as a vital link in an evangelistic chain. When you can visualize Sunday School's part in grafting newcomers, it can have a great impact on the growth of your church. Here are some ways that you can utilize its ministry:

1. *Urge everyone to attend Sunday School.* Let it be known that Sunday School is one of the most viable opportunities for spiritual growth. Give it prominence. Organize it, advertise it and emphasize it. If it's not prominent in the calendar and in the bulletin, it won't be prominent in people's memory. Communicate the spiritual benefits of Sunday School. Help your congregation understand that it is a place where people can personally encounter Christ—and where seeking hearts can find that special friend who's been looking for them all along.
2. *Promote the use of Sunday School for evangelism.* Let your teachers understand the evangelistic purpose of their ministry. Make Sunday School an integral part of the church's game plan. Use staff meetings to convey the church's primary purpose of leading people to a saving knowledge of Christ.
3. *Designate "Salvation Sunday"* as a special Sunday when every teacher will offer an invitation to salvation in his

or her class. Give attendees an opportunity to respond to the gospel message. Encourage your teaching staff to move beyond "reading the menu" and reciting the "daily specials" to "taking the order." As the unsaved come to know Jesus Christ, they will naturally move into the mainstream of the local church ministry. And the result will be church growth.

4. *Celebrate victories.* Record the results of your evangelistic outreach and celebrate success at your staff meetings. The Bible tells us that angels rejoice over the salvation of one soul (see Luke 15:7). Take their cue. Throw a little praise party in your next organizational meeting. It will not only lift morale, but it will also serve as a reminder of the core values of your ministry.

▼——————————————————————————

How many unsaved people attend your church? How many avenues into their lives do you have? Sunday School is one more. It is the nonthreatening atmosphere in which they can be invited to accept Christ.

Action Point: What will it take to incorporate Sunday School into the evangelistic ministry of your church?

Chapter 2

SUNDAY SCHOOL WILL GIVE YOU EXTRA DOORS INTO THE CHURCH

"I can't believe the number of people who are here!" exclaimed Janet, a longtime member of Trinity Wesleyan Church. Then she asked, "Do they all belong to *our* church?"

The multipurpose room was bustling with children and parents, young adults and seniors for Trinity Wesleyan's "pitch in" dinner. Since the church had added a third worship service in September, there had been few occasions when the whole church family got together.

"They are our enlarged church family," Pastor Kline said excitedly.

"But where did they all come from? I mean, adding a single worship service couldn't account for all this growth." Janet couldn't help but wonder what had changed. She was used to the old days when she knew everyone at church suppers by name.

"But our church didn't just add one extra service," said Pastor Kline. "We added a lot of new doors in order that visitors might come into our church."

Janet knew the pastor was not talking about renovations to the church building. He meant additional opportunities for people to come to the church. So Janet asked her pastor to tell her about them.

"When we added the Saturday evening worship service," he began, "we also added three Sunday School classes. Now, we have additional Sunday School classes for kids; we have a class for divorce recovery, one for new converts and one on understanding Christianity and Islam. And besides those, we have a support group for single moms and a class for couples expecting their first child."

Janet was astonished. "You mean people have started attending the church because of new classes in Sunday School?"

"Why not?" Pastor Kline smiled. "Each of these new classes meets a need in people's lives. We're offering them something they need, socially, emotionally and spiritually—but each class touches people at a different level."

"Oh, I forgot one class," Pastor Kline said with a twinkle in his eye. The wise pastor knew that Janet had grown up in the church and liked the Bible basics. "We have an elective Bible class that teaches Bible survey. It seems a lot of new people want to learn the fundamentals of the Bible."

"This is wonderful," Janet sighed. "Maybe there are more new things in our church than just the praise choruses we sing in worship."

A Balanced Diet

No single ministry of your church will reach everyone. It's true that many people are attracted to the dynamic atmosphere of a vibrant worship service. But as Janet noted, there's more to church ministry than upbeat singing. The Sunday-morning sermon alone doesn't fully equip the saint—it's not enough. And listening to a sermon doesn't necessarily result in learning. Rather, it's *involvement* that equals learning. The small-group classes in Sunday School offer a balanced diet. Face-to-face interaction in the Word of God is the great hope of the church.

Every church needs a variety of ministries that touch people at different levels. Sunday School provides these various and creative opportunities for involvement. The more *entrance points*—doors—a church has, the more people it will attract.

Action Point: Make a list of the doors into your church. What were the last doors you added? How effective have they been in helping your church reach new people?

Doors of Opportunity

Sunday School offers more potential entrance points than any other ministry. The varieties of personalized ministries that it can offer are outstanding. The following are some doors you can add to your church through Sunday School.

Age-Graded Doors

People like to be among their peers. Sunday School naturally brings together teens with teens, young adults with young adults, seniors with seniors, singles with singles. Children in similar age groups develop fast friendships and develop a connection with Sunday School early in life. Adding an age- or stage-of-life-specific class is an opportunity to minister to a variety of people.

Teaching Doors

Acts 2:42 reminds us that the apostles' teaching was another foundation stone of the Church. People are hungry for sound Bible teaching, and the Sunday School is the perfect setting to allow you to meet that need. Through graded curricula, students will have the opportunity to study the entire Bible over a period of several years. And the corporate study of the Word will also give them spiritual armor against the false teaching that is so prevalent these days.

Fellowship Doors

The smaller the group, the greater the intimacy. Sunday School, with its naturally developed small groups, provides one of the best venues for fellowship in any church. Often the love of Christ is communicated *before* or *after* the class session, as well as *during* the class. Jesus taught His disciples about the worth of giving even a cup of cold water. Modern disciples have added the coffeepot. Sit the average American male in a straight-back Sunday School chair, with the traditional teacher lecture, and he's not going to say much, if anything at all. But put a cup of coffee in a young father's hand, sit him in a circle of guys and ask him about his favorite team; he'll speak up. When you've got the guy interested, ask him about his frustrations; then show him how God makes a difference.

Teens love fellowship. Most of them would rather stand in the hall and talk to their buddies than sit in a class listening to a lecture. Build fellowship into class time. Let it flow naturally into class time. Build teen loyalty on natural discussions of the Word of God.

Lifelong friendships are formed in a Sunday School class and life lessons are learned through questions that force people to study the Bible. People are looking for someone to *care about their cares*—thus opening a door of fellowship into the church.

Action Point: Are your classes taking advantage of fellowship in Sunday School?

Special-Interest Doors

Who wrote the Bible? When will Jesus return? What does the Bible say about our money management? Inquiring minds want to know. Vibrant Sunday Schools are learning centers where some of the most important questions in life are answered in a friendly and informative way. Specialty classes also offer a nonthreatening environment for those struggling with personal or social issues.

Massive changes in society may require similar changes in the local church. Who knows what's next! Three-and-a-half-day workweeks? What about the extended weekend? How will the church compete with the continuing growth of recreation? Obviously, innovative programs will be necessary if new people are to visit your church.

▼ ———————————————————————————————

E xtra doors are needed—right now. Spirit-led ministries that meet the spiritual and social needs of senior adults, middle-aged adults, young adults, singles, teens and children are as close as your next planning meeting.

How many doors does your church have? How many ways do you have to mainstream people into your church ministry? The more the better! Use Sunday School to create new entry points to your congregation.

Action Point: Brainstorm with your staff to double the number of doors your church could potentially add in the near future.

Chapter 3

SUNDAY SCHOOL WILL BOOST BIBLE KNOWLEDGE

"Pastor, I need to speak with you." Ryan Thompson sounded upset. A computer programmer with an $80,000 annual income, this young professional was a leader among the young adults at Immanuel Church.

"What's the problem?" Pastor Kohler asked brightly.

"This!" said Ryan, holding up a copy of *Turmoil*, a million-selling novel about the end times. "I just finished reading about the Second Coming, and it's terrifying! Did you know that the Spirit Jesus has already returned to Earth? It says here that demonic agents are in control of Egypt, Japan and Argentina. The Battle of Armageddon will take place in Africa sometime before 2010."

Then with a trace of accusation in his voice, Ryan pleaded, "How come you never told me about this?"

Pastor Kohler shook his head. *How could this bright young man be so easily deceived?* He thought, *Doesn't he know anything about the Bible?* He answered, "The story is much more exciting than that! You hold a fictitious hypothesis, whereas the Bible tells of true—and scary—future events. Didn't you learn that in Sunday School?"

"I've never been to Sunday School," he replied. "Isn't Sunday School for kids?"

Biblical literacy is at an all-time low, even among churched people. Many don't even know the most basic stories of the Bible. Blank stares accompany a reference to David and Goliath. To some church members, Daniel in the lion's den could be a reference to someone's membership in a service club!

Most modern church services don't include a lot of Bible teaching. Modern worship services include Scripture readings, and the sermons are aimed at helping worshipers deal with the issues of life. But it seems modern people don't want to listen to theological explanations in their sermons. So where is the modern Christian taught the essentials of Christianity?

Lack of biblical knowledge leaves Christ's flock with no depth to their personal faith. This, in turn, makes them vulnerable to the aggressive "evangelism" of those practicing Islam, Buddhism and Mormonism. Will failure to impart Bible knowledge leave church members ripe for deception?

Action Point: If all your members' knowledge about the Bible was learned from your sermons, how much would they know?

Built-In Bible Study

The good news is that nearly every church has a built-in Bible-teaching ministry—Sunday School! The vehicle for countering false teaching with the truth is already in place.

Your church has the exciting opportunity of raising the level of Bible knowledge. In order to help you, publishing houses of most denominations have a storehouse of material that will lead inquiring minds on a journey through the truth of the Bible—from Genesis to Revelation.

And no other teaching venue is as versatile. Aside from the wide variety of teaching techniques that a Sunday School teacher uses, the curriculum itself employs a variety of methods.

1. *Doctrinal.* A study of the Bible (all or part) to see the development of great Christian teachings such as sin, grace and salvation.
2. *Biographical.* A study of one or more biblical characters, like Abraham, David or Peter.
3. *Devotional.* A study tracing key points of personal spirituality such as prayer and practicing the presence of God.
4. *Historical.* A look at how God has been at work throughout Bible history and Church history.
5. *Prophetical.* The study of God's plan for the future.
6. *Topical.* The study of any given topic—war, divorce, money, homosexuality—from a biblical point of view.

Action Point: What is the strongest contribution of your Sunday School's teaching ministry? The weakest?

Battle Against False Teaching

The pastor who awakens the "sleeping giant" of Sunday School and plans for aggressive Bible teaching will arm his or her church with biblically literate Christians. And armed they must be! As Tim LaHaye once advised us, "The battle for the mind is being waged."[1] The enemy has spent millions on the publishing and advertisement of its principles. Yet the Church on the whole has failed to prepare its members for this worldly onslaught: Biblically illiterate Christians are sitting ducks.

Even the lines of faith are becoming increasingly blurred because of this dangerous illiteracy. Universalism is creeping under the front doors of the Lord's House. The "all roads lead to heaven" prophets are energetically—and often effectively—trying to convince believers of their pluralistic doctrine. But the standard is clearly marked in the Scriptures: "Salvation is found in no one else, for there is no other name under heaven given to men by which we must be saved" (Acts 4:12, author's translation). Jesus is, and will forever be, the path to heaven.

Action Point: What "false teaching" has recently affected members of your church? How did you deal with the problem? How could you have prevented the problem?

Sunday School's New Mission

Pastor, you have the opportunity to raise the bar. It is the church's job to arm its members with the truth in order to withstand the fiery darts of hell's forces. Give your Sunday School department a new mission within this job. And commission your staff as soldiers in the war on biblical ignorance.

Set the standard.

Open the pages of God's Word to your audience weekly (not weakly). Let biblical principles take precedence over popular ideas; memorize the Scriptures; quote from the Scriptures; illustrate with Scriptures; use Scriptures in your church publications; read from the Scriptures in your worship service. When it comes to Bible knowledge, all eyes are on the pulpit.

Plan your attack.
Watch over your curriculum like a hawk. Make sure there is a systematic teaching of God's Word. Offer exciting electives that focus on the Bible.

Ask questions.
Use your pulpit to ask the hard questions about current issues. Let questions be like salt on the tongue—making people thirsty for Bible knowledge. Only God's Word can satisfy. Only God's Word can answer the foundational issues of life.

Teach the teachers.
Make sure those who stand before your classes or small groups have adequate knowledge of the Word—and know how to "rightly divide" it (see 2 Tim. 2:15). Offer Bible survey classes as a teacher-training curriculum, and equip your staff with library resources.

Celebrate successes.
Give assignments, and then acknowledge publicly those who have reached goals of Scripture reading or memorization.

Biblically Literate Children

Adults in your congregation need to know the message, details and promises of the Bible—this is quite clear. But there is a way to begin educating Christians before they become biblically illiterate adults. Children's Sunday School classes will play a huge role in the development of a young mind. With biblically sound curriculum and knowledgeable teachers, children in your church can *start* with a correct and exciting view of the Bible.

What a way to build strong Christians who can face the world that is waiting to deceive them! Don't wait for church members to become illiterate before educating them; while still young, raise them to read the Word.

▼ ───────────────────────────────────────

A stable population of mature believers will be virtually immune to error, confident to take their faith into the world and "equipped for every good work" (2 Tim. 3:17).

Action Point: What do you want your church to be like five years from now in biblical competency?

Chapter 4

Sunday School
Will Help
You Minister to
All Ages

"I'm sorry, Pastor. We really love your preaching, but our family needs to be somewhere else right now." Dave Thomason had been in the church for six years, having joined the church with his wife and two elementary-school children. They had been faithful workers in the church. Now Dave felt a responsibility to tell his pastor that his family was leaving.

Pastor Tim was shocked. Since his appointment to Epworth Church two years before, he'd bent over backward to be all things to all people (see 1 Cor. 9:22). He made pastoral visits to the nursing home twice a month and met regularly with the church's children. His wife, Debbie, even staffed the nursery—almost single-handedly—for nearly every worship service. He didn't have the time—or the energy—to add another ministry.

"It's our kids," Dave continued. "They're now teenagers, and Epworth really doesn't have a ministry for them. We need a church that has something for our whole family, so we're going to Southlawn—they have an active Sunday School for teens." Dave continued with a trace of sadness in his voice, "I know you're trying, Pastor Tim, but our kids—they're at a very crucial age."

Pastor Tim's heart sank as he fought back the tears. *What more can I do?* he wondered. *What more can I do?*

Action Point: Do you know people who have left your church because it didn't have a program for them? What were they looking for? Make a list.

Moving Targets

Sunday School is the undervalued resource of most congregations. It has been quietly ministering to all age groups for more than 200 years. While strategists tinker with new models for reaching the latest demographic target, Sunday School is right there—usually with a class already serving the target group.

Some church leaders want to add additional ministries to help the church—home Bible classes, seminars, weekend retreats, gym nights, etc. But most Americans need extra meetings like they need a Band-Aid on a bowling ball. Most Americans are too busy to attend another meeting—so why add something new to their already busy schedules? Your people are already driving to church, so make use of Sunday School.

And no ministry is easier to expand than Sunday School. Adding a class or changing its focus means recruiting or retraining only one leader. The infrastructure is already there (for more guidelines and ideas for effective Sunday School classes of all ages, see *How to Have a Great Sunday School* by Wes and Sheryl Haystead, Gospel Light, 2000).

Here are some of the target groups your Sunday School can easily reach.

1. *Age groups*. This is the most common arrangement of Sunday School classes. Each class targets a different age level.
2. *Life-stage groups*. These classes attract people in common life stages, regardless of age: single, divorced, empty nest, caregiver.
3. *Need-based groups*. People gather based on a current need in their lives, such as grief recovery, marriage preparation, parenthood, etc. These are usually short-term classes.
4. *Interest groups*. These classes gather people with a common interest. In most cases, this will be some biblical topic such as prophecy or cults. Some classes are organized around people with a common hobby—skateboarding, camping or quilting.

Action Point: What groups are strongest in your church? What groups are weakest?

Pastor Hercules

Worship alone doesn't cross the interest or attention barriers. Preparing one sermon for every age group is a Herculean task—and Hercules probably didn't have a seminary degree. Retention is as much of a challenge as attention. To cut across all age-group lines with a single message would probably cut into the after-church restaurant time—it would simply take too long to present.

But, pastors, you *can* preach to every age level at once. How? Through your Sunday School teachers! Your trained Sunday School staff takes the message of the gospel into the classroom and affects the entire congregation at every spiritual, emotional or physical level. This multiplies and enhances your ministry at the same time that it gives doses of truth that fit the listener's maturity.

That principle alone takes at least one burden off your shoulders. If you were the sole communicator—if the Sunday morning or evening message were the only means of conveying biblical truth—yours would be a worrisome task. Sunday School gives you an added voice, another arm and greater means to meet the spiritual needs of your congregation. What you could never teach because of some barrier or stereotype, your trained

> *The trained Sunday School staff affects the entire congregation at every spiritual, emotional and physical level.*

Sunday School staff member can communicate. Lay ministry staff don't have to scale the same walls as vocational ministers.

The mechanism is already in place. It may need a little retooling or a little oiling, but it's all there. You have a valuable method for teaching eternal truth to people at all intervals of the spiritual journey.

Action Point: What is a burden in your ministry that Sunday School could help?

A Place for the Prodigal

Sunday School also complements other small-group ministries. Many unchurched (or even churched) adults in your community have been trained to go to Sunday School as part of a childhood routine. But they have dropped out. They are like the Prodigal Son. And as soon as the need for the spiritual becomes obvious, seekers will return to their roots. You might as well hang a "Welcome" sign at the door of your Christian education center, because that's where the prodigals will eventually feel most at home. When they think *I need to get back to church*, Sunday School is probably the first thing that comes to mind.

Bigger churches need on-site little churches to retain congregants. The same people who get "lost in the crowd" get "found" in a small group. The common interest or maturity level that draws people to small groups (such as a Sunday School class) makes them feel at home once they get there. Whether it's a Bible study, musical group, training group or Sunday School class, people need to feel welcomed at a personal-interest level.

Are you looking to reach a target group? You may not need a new ministry. The oldest ministry in your church will probably do the job—Sunday School.

Action Point: What thought have you given to getting prodigals back into your church/Sunday School?

Chapter 5

SUNDAY SCHOOL
WILL HELP YOU
MEET NEEDS

"It's not his fault," Laura, a recent new member, added quickly as she talked with the wife of her Sunday School teacher. "I just wouldn't feel comfortable talking to the pastor about this. I mean—my problem is really more of a . . . woman's problem."

Stephanie Powell's husband had taught Sunday School for years. Her new friend, Laura Green, had been attending Liberty Church for about three months and had a problem that a man couldn't handle. Stephanie sensed she could help, so she decided to invite Laura out for coffee.

"Infertility is not a shameful thing," Stephanie offered gently. "And you might be surprised at the number of women affected by it. Like miscarriage and even rape—it happens more often than you might think."

"I know," Laura sighed, staring into her coffee cup. "But still, I wish there was someplace I could share with other women about it—privately. I mean, without men around."

Stephanie smiled, thinking of the "For Women Only" Sunday School class she'd be starting in two weeks. "I know just the place," she said.

People are suffering in your church. Every gathering of people contains some who are suffering from grief, infidelity, illness, divorce or abuse. And then there are those who are just plain stressed out. As a pastor, you can't counsel every person in crisis. Even if they would come for counseling (and many won't), you simply don't have the time to see all of them and address every point of need.

And you can't preach a sermon on every specific problem. Your service would become a niche, aimed to a few and missing many—or boring them. A special problem sermon might hit a few, but you'd lose others simply because you don't know their particular needs.

Outpatient Clinic

Sunday School can help. This ministry is a network of support groups where people can find counsel, support and fellowship while facing nearly any problem. The high intimacy and high accountability of the Sunday School class makes sharing possible and authentic caring certain.

Here's what you can do to make your Sunday School an outpatient clinic for hurting souls.

Use the 50-50 plan.
Be sure your teachers understand that building a caring fellowship is one-half of a class's purpose. Bible teaching is the other half. Many classes emphasize Bible teaching at the expense of caring fellowship. Good

teachers fully devote half of their class time to sharing and caring.

Promote follow-up.
Fellowship doesn't end when the bell rings. Urge teachers (and students) to follow up on the needs that are identified during class time. Phone calls, e-mails and notes of encouragement should be common. Providing meals, child care, respite care and rides to the doctor should also be normal activities.

Utilize special classes.
Offer classes targeted at special needs such as divorce recovery, grief or caregiving. You might be surprised to find qualified professionals in the congregation who would gladly give of their time and experience in teaching a short-term class on special needs.

Offer your facilities.
There may be a Christian support group in your community that needs a meeting place. By offering your facilities, you are not only helping the community group, you are adding a ministry—without charge or added staffing. The additional on-site ministry might also be a feeder to your Sunday School, small group or worship crowd. Familiarity doesn't necessarily breed contempt—it often breeds interest.

Use professionals as adjunct teachers.
A four-week class on a timely topic will not only meet needs, it will also serve as another door of welcome. The value of having a professional teach a short course and meet needs will make it worth the extra effort.

Action Point: Brainstorm with your staff and congregation about programs that could be added to make Sunday School more of a help-giving agency.

Jethro Principle

Remember Jethro? Moses got a lecture about being Mr. Everything from his father-in-law. Moses was advised to delegate much of his tasks to others in the camp. Sunday School is the *Jethro principle* in action. The ministerial staff can't be everywhere at once. And about the time they're over here, someone over there will need them. People with needs don't like to be ignored—no matter what they say to the contrary. The very person who is encouraging you to take care of someone else first is probably churning inside over his or her own hurts not being tended to—it's just a fact of life.

But what you can't do in your own strength, you can do in the Sunday School. You can create an oasis of compassion and caring—and put it on the calendar. Your Sunday School may not be what the doctor ordered, but with a little bit of effort, Sunday School can *become* the doctor. Your staff can be trained to look, listen and pray for the needs of the greater church community.

▼———————————————————

You can only counsel one person at a time. But your Sunday School can offer support to dozens of hurting people each week. Why not use it?

Action Point: What can you say in your sermons to create a church-wide concern for offering unique help to individuals through the Sunday School?

Chapter 6

SUNDAY SCHOOL WILL PRODUCE LEADERS IN YOUR CHURCH

"There's no way," Ron said flatly. "I can't help you with this class—I'm not a teacher."

Ron Weekly was retired and had plenty of time on his hands, but he'd been a pew sitter at Union Church ever since he'd joined. Phil Hughes, the Sunday School superintendent, had asked his friend Ron to help out with the junior boys' class.

"Who said anything about teaching?" Phil countered, "I just need some help."

"Forget it," Ron insisted. "I've never taught anyone to do anything."

The superintendent knew better. Ever since he got out of military service, Ron had been a tool and die maker at a local machine shop, managing and training the employees.

"Look, Ron, I'm not asking you to speak in public or present Bible lessons. I just need some help with the grunt work."

"Such as?"

"Easy stuff. Setting up the room, making reminder phone calls to our regulars, enlisting volunteers to help on our outings—things like that."

"Really? That's all?"

"No," the honest Sunday School superintendent confessed. "I also need you to sit in the back of the room to keep rambunctious boys still."

"Sure," Ron agreed. "Those are little things; I can do them."

"Good," Phil smiled. "That's the way I got started serving the Lord. I also served as the assistant to the junior boys' class!"

Phil then shared with Ron how before that he had never done anything for God in the church; but when he began working with junior boys, he got a sense of satisfaction when he saw God working in their lives.

"And now I need an assistant," said Phil, finishing his story. "And God can use you!"

"OK," Ron said. "If that's all I have to do."

"That's all," Phil said with a smile. "For now."

The Leadership Chain

Sunday School is a prep school for church leaders. Those who serve in this ministry receive mentoring, skill training, personal development and ministry preparation that they won't get anywhere else outside of seminary. Sunday School workers become Sunday School leaders. Then Sunday School leaders become church leaders.

But leadership skills aren't the only things they learn. Think of the spiritual lessons that leaders experience as they help lead a class. When they face a tough situation, they pray; so future leaders learn to trust God to solve problems. Remember, you've got to grow the faith of future leaders because, "Without faith it is impossible to please [God]" (Heb. 11:6).

Also, Sunday School helpers are asked questions—all kinds of questions—by students who want answers. And they want answers now, not later. So helpers have to know the Bible and they have to be able to tell students how God works in everyday life. "But sanctify the Lord God in your hearts, and always be ready to give [an answer] to everyone who asks you" (2 Pet. 3:15). Therefore, as your congregants begin helping in Sunday School, they will automatically grow in maturity and leadership ability.

The classic chain of leadership is outlined in the familiar letter of the apostle Paul to Pastor Timothy: "And the things that you have heard from me among many witnesses, commit these to faithful men who will be able to teach others also" (2 Tim. 2:2). The future of the Church was at stake. Its global and community impact was on the line. Paul knew that unless a teacher-mentoring program was put in place, the ball would be dropped—and scores of people would live and die without knowing the Lord Jesus Christ. Too much was on the line to let the "gospel ship" sail without biblical leadership. It still is!

Action Point: Brainstorm with your staff to come up with a list of leaders in your church who have grown into their place of leadership by first serving in entry-level capacities.

Sunday School Leadership Skills

Sunday School is a natural choice for training and nurturing leaders. Here are some vital skills that Sunday School leaders acquire.

Administration

Each class is a unit with the teacher as leader. The class deals in miniature with nearly every facet of church life—attendance, recruitment, finances, event planning, crisis management, time management, resource management and personnel counseling. Sunday School teachers must learn to manage their group, yet never with a distant attitude. They must love their curriculum (the Bible), love their students, love God and love the work of God.

Evangelism

Sunday School is an evangelistic ministry; therefore, teachers must never adopt a "maintenance" attitude. They must encourage their students to share Christ with their friends. They must contact prospects to get them into the class. They must contact visitors to get them to return. Just as every living thing grows and bears fruit, so must the Sunday School class. It is the job of the teacher to plant the seed and nurture it. Then in God's harvest, many are added to the Kingdom (see chapter 19, "Friendship Evangelism").

Sunday School teachers can learn to become comfortable with presenting the plan of salvation, individually and to the group, even if they don't feel particularly gifted in this area.

People Skills

The incessant talker. The know-it-all. The complainer. The late arriver. These are a few of the usual characters in any class—or in any church. Sunday School leaders grow as they develop tact in handling these problem people and the difficult situations they often create.

Whole-Church Vision

Sunday School gives a vision for the entire church and its ministry. Sunday School leaders become the pastor's allies in advancing the entire ministry of the church and promoting vital community. They will advertise special church events and attend along with their pupils.

Mentoring Opportunities

The Sunday School ministry has built-in mentoring opportunities. The pastor mentors the superintendent. The superintendent mentors department leaders. Department leaders mentor teachers. Teachers mentor assistants. Assistants mentor pupils, as do all of the above. Remember, we are workmen together with God (see 1 Cor. 3:9).

Action Point: What is the strongest characteristic of the leaders who have been trained in your church?

Potential Leaders

The church could triple its effectiveness if it could double its number of leaders. One Christian educator wrote,

> Too many churches still place people in positions and hope for the best. Evangelical congregations must approach the task armed with a philosophy of ministry that honors the work of the Lord and allows people to be fulfilled in ministry. No longer can they merely run programs; they must help people develop their spiritual gifts and be sensitive to a mutual ministry to and in the body.[1]

There is a leader-training school already in place in your church. Week after week, local churches are actually training leaders through Sunday School ministries. From the superintendent to the department leaders to the teaching staff, scores of potential leaders are being developed to serve God.

Once a simple bricklayer, who had been a pew warmer his whole life, was asked to help keep discipline in the back of the room in a church in Indianapolis. As this bricklayer tried to keep the boys quiet, he bluntly told the teacher, "No wonder the boys cut up—the lesson is boring!" Next week the bricklayer told the Bible story, using the rough English of a construction worker. The boys sat transfixed. When the junior girls heard about his storytelling ability, he was asked to speak in opening assembly, telling both boys and girls the Bible story. He became so comfortable in front of a group that he ended up speaking to the whole Sunday School—and over 1,000 people were in attendance!

The leadership ability he developed in Sunday School spilled over into his job. His Sunday School confidence motivated him to begin his own construction firm. First 1 house, then 3, next 14, and finally he ended up building a subdivision of homes. He testified, "I'd still be a common bricklayer if Sunday School leadership hadn't pushed me to think big, plan big and put a lot of people to work."

Does it pay to train bricklayers to be leaders? His pastor showed me a photocopy of a tithe check the bricklayer gave to the church after his company completed work on a federal building in Washington, D.C. It was written in the amount of $252,000!

Pastor, by developing leaders, you have the opportunity to directly influence the future of your church, the future of your church members' lives and the future of the kingdom of God. You will build the character of the leaders you recruit, and your passion will become their passion; your attitude will be reflected in their attitudes. As you lead, so will they. You are primarily responsible for the developing of leaders for future generations.

And what better place to launch that leader development than in your Sunday School? Remember, people learn to lead by leading. They learn what not to do from their mistakes, and they learn what to do from their successes. So let's train leaders. You can jump-start your leaders by using this book as a tool and remind them of the importance of Sunday School. Develop leaders who love to teach the Word and fellowship with God's people.

Curriculum has already been written. Classroom sites have already been built. Mentors are standing by. And pupils or staff members are ready to follow those who will lead.

The Kingdom still needs a few good men (and women)! And the Sunday School is still one of the best boot camps.

Action Point: What area in your church has had the strongest influence in leadership training? Why?

Chapter 7

SUNDAY SCHOOL WILL PROVIDE ROLE MODELS

"Can I, Dad? Can I? Huh? Huh?"

"Ask your mother!" John Somerville replied impatiently. He was frustrated with his son's persistent pleading to go to a Sunday School pizza party, so he sent his son, Taylor, to ask his mother.

"Can I, Mom? Come on. Can I go?" Taylor was persistent and wouldn't give up.

"Taylor, please wait a minute!" Debbie tried to keep her son quiet—with little success. Finally, she asked her husband, "What's gotten into this kid?"

The Somervilles could have had worse problems. Nine-year-old Taylor was simply excited about the pizza party for his Sunday School class. His teacher had told Taylor he needed permission to attend. So Taylor was determined to keep asking until he got what he wanted.

"It's the pizza party, John," Debbie explained. "Taylor's been talking about it for days."

"I know," her husband responded. "But why is he so interested in church all of a sudden? Last week it was memory verses. The week before it was a Bible scavenger hunt. What gives?"

His wife smiled and said two words: "Dave Lilly." Dave was the high school sophomore who'd been enlisted as the assistant teacher for the fourth-grade class. He had taken Taylor under his wing.

Debbie continued her explanation: "And all the younger kids look up to Dave Lilly. He's a great role model for the boys." She smiled, looking at Taylor, who had been waiting, breathlessly, for the jury's verdict.

"Can I go, Dad? Can I?"

John thought a minute. "You know, Debbie, this is a lot better than his asking to hang out at the mall." In the end, John not only agreed to let Taylor go, he also volunteered to take Taylor to the pizza party himself.

The greatest testimony to the importance of Sunday School can be seen in the lives of the students who have been influenced by the Word of God. Once students have heard our Lord calling them, they can reach out to accept the invitation that He offers. It is then that Sunday School bears the only kind of fruit that really matters in the end. Michael J. Anthony puts it this way: "The only fruit which will last for eternity is that of people whose lives have been brought into relationship with God in Christ and whose lives reflect the risen Lord."[1]

Your Sunday School has the capacity to influence lives in many ways: through the lessons heard, the applications given, the stories told, the creative learning activities in which students participate and the Bible verses learned. But one of the greatest influences of your Sunday School is the model of your Sunday School staff.

Instant Role Models

Role models—good and bad—are everywhere. Each day, society sets in front of your church members examples of conduct and character. Business leaders, fashion models, actors, athletes—some of them are good models, but many aren't.

Worldly role models are influential because they often spend more time with your church members than you do, Pastor! You have approximately two to four hours each week to influence your congregants through teaching and preaching ministries. Sometimes you can increase the amount of one-on-one contact if you visit them in their homes or make yourself available to them through various ministries. But no matter how hard you try, it will still probably be true that media and sports personalities will have many more hours to mold the minds and hearts of those under your charge than you do.

You've heard the expression "We need more models than critics." That's very true. But where are those *positive* models to be found? Who will be the person or persons who will lead others to a positive and powerful relationship with Christ? The answer: the Sunday School workers in your church.

Sunday School workers are instant role models. Ideally, they're chosen based on their yieldedness to God, maturity and spiritual gifts. As workers grow in Christ, they become role models to everyone in the church, especially those to whom they minister.

Action Point: Ask your staff members who their Christian heroes and heroines were when growing up. Why? Were any Sunday School leaders?

The Hall of Fame

Who are the heroes in your church? Whose lives are lifted up as examples for your children, your teens, your young adults, your married couples or your senior adults? Who are the most influential people in your church? Probably your church members would point to a Sunday School leader or teacher—past or present. Scores of people have been brought into the Kingdom because of a faithful teacher or department leader. And each of us would add a name or two of a Sunday School worker onto the list concerning those who have directly influenced our lives. The ranks of ministry have been filled with people who are directly or indirectly the product of some faithful Sunday School staff member.

But you might be wondering how to ensure that your Sunday School is staffed with heroes. Follow the lead

The ranks of ministry have been filled with people who are directly or indirectly the product of some faithful Sunday School staff member.

of Samuel: Listen to God as he speaks through your pastoral staff and your congregation. Be looking for those who have outstanding influence and the potential to bring others into a vital relationship with the Lord. Look for men and women who, like David, have a heart for God. See as God sees (see 1 Sam. 16:7). Give these candidates the opportunity to lead. They will become great heroes for the young in your church.

Action Point: Who are the role models for the youth in your church? Ask some of the youth of your church who their choice might be, and why. Did you choose the same or different role models?

Character Bank

Sunday School can become a "character bank" of your church. Staff members, prayerfully selected, trained and appointed, can very well be those who influence church growth. Today, people are searching for a genuine warmth. They need to see a religion that has some fire in its hearth. No matter their background, seekers who are looking for a vital relationship with their creator want to clasp hands with someone who knows Him in a personal way. In one very real sense, the numerical growth of your church is dependent on the spiritual growth of its core constituency.

▼

Sunday School is an ideal place to put the lives of victorious Christians on display. Whether in the office or in the classroom, those who model the attitudes of Christ will have an eternal impact on those who are looking for Him from whom all good things come.

Action Point: For your church to become truly healthy, it needs healthy Christians who will lift up their brothers and sisters. How can you make this happen?

Chapter 8

SUNDAY SCHOOL WILL TURN SPECTATORS INTO WORKERS

"Michelle, our new church is *f-a-a-bulous!*" Kelley, your typical yuppie, gushed. "We finally found everything we're looking for." Kelley's husband just grinned and nodded his approval.

Kelley and Michelle were casually chatting at their son's T-ball game when the topic of church came up. That's when Kelley raved about their new church. Michelle knew that Kelley and her husband had browsed several congregations over the years—some call it church hopping. Lately Kelley and her husband had been attending Day Spring Church, a new congregation on the north side of town that featured contemporary worship.

"I hear their advertisements on the radio," Michelle said. "What's it like?"

Kelley began to brag about her new church. "It's too *fabulous*! The worship band is *so* hot. And they do a little bit of drama every week; they have Starbucks coffee in the lounge; they provide the most marvelous child care; they—"

"Sounds great," Michelle interrupted. "And what do you do at Day Spring?"

Kelley seemed puzzled by the question.

"I mean your ministry," said Michelle. "I keep hearing about the things *they* do. But what do *you* do?"

Kelley stared. "Michelle, darling, we *attend*. What else *would* we do?"

Sunday School Employment Agency

Some churches have congregations that resemble an audience attending a sporting event or a concert. They show up to watch, cheer and perhaps boo (sometimes they even buy a ticket), but they never leave their seats to be part of the action. Sunday School puts these people to work. It trains them for ministry, makes them accountable and motivates them to achieve. Sunday School turns the *organism* of the church into an *organized*, serving body.

Here are five things you'll seldom hear at a church with a thriving Sunday School.

1. *That's not my job.* Sunday School leaders usually pitch in.
2. *We can't afford it.* Sunday School leaders usually find a way to get things done.
3. *I'm too busy.* Sunday School leaders were all busy people *before* they became leaders. They're used to managing multiple priorities.

4. *I don't know how.* Sunday School leaders have learned by doing. They know they can handle the challenge of acquiring a new skill.

5. *It's not my turn.* Sunday School leaders are team players.

Sunday School has a job for everyone, and everyone should have a job.

Action Point: What's the difference between pastoring a megachurch in which the pastoral staff does most of the ministry and a small church in which most of the congregation is involved in every level of ministry?

A Good Place to Start

Nothing seems to be the same in *churchdom*. Societal changes have most certainly affected the ministry of the local church. Even generational differences come into play. Sunday School can be a stabilizing force, actually turning negative trends into a positive. Steve Rabey writes, "Many members of the emerging generations of Christians have almost totally forsaken the public square to focus on ministry within the church context."[1]

As long as folks are sitting idly in the pews, why not put them to work? And Sunday School is a good place to start. Some attendees, who would go into cardiac arrest if they had to stand in front of a group, would actually jump at the chance to sit in the back row and possibly act as a "stabilizer" for some attention-craving second grader in a Sunday School class.

Part of the joy of ministry is finding the right place for people (based on their natural skills) and then putting them in their place. Williams and Gangel advise,

A larger percentage of people are not involved in church ministry because they have not been taught to understand the true nature of the church. Church leaders must understand this lack and work to overcome it. We must reverse the "too-much-on-too-few" syndrome; it leads to burnout and ineffective ministry. The alternative is to share leadership with others who will feel a part of the total ministry and be fulfilled in serving the Lord.[2]

Action Point: Examine the conduit that your church uses to get prospective leaders out of the pew and into active ministry. Does your church have a systematic conduit that is working? Why or why not?

Supply and Demand

The new emphasis on multiple services exacerbates the need for more workers. It means multiple ushers, multiple choirs and multiple support personnel. But more important, multiple services most often means multiple Sunday Schools or small-group meetings. New teachers and leaders must be found, trained and given a room assignment. But keep in mind that the *demand* is a great boon to the *supply*. Sunday School growth naturally calls for more training. And training gives prominence to natural leaders.

Out of a six-week training course, one or more natural-born leaders will be identified. The next task for the ministry staff is to find a place of leadership for those naturals. A department. A class. An assistant's position. Find the perfect match and you will help your church—and greatly enhance the spiritual growth of that individual.

Once again, Sunday School is a great "feeder" for church leadership. The skills that are developed there will be skills that can be used in other areas of church leadership. Sunday School is great internship training.

Kelley and Jeff found an exciting *church* at Day Spring Church, but they will never find their *church home* until they find a place of service. Pastor, you have some couples like Kelley and Jeff in your church. You can help them find their place. Start with the Sunday School. Give them a place to serve. It will not only help them in their spiritual growth, but it will also serve as a the glue that binds them to the house of God.

Does your church consist of 200 people badly in need of exercise watching 20 people badly in need of rest? Sunday School will turn those numbers around.

Action Point: Brainstorm with your staff and compile a list of prospective leaders who are not involved at present. What will it take to get them involved?

Chapter 9

SUNDAY SCHOOL WILL PROVIDE PRAYER INTERCESSORS

"So it's definitely cancer?" Catherine asked gently.

Marjorie Edler nodded tearfully. She couldn't bring herself even to say the *C* word. Her husband, Bert, had died of colon cancer five years ago. They'd barely retired when he began fighting the disease. Now Marjorie had her own battle to fight. "I didn't want to tell the whole church, Catherine—but I thought you should know."

"Marjorie, I'm taking this news to our Sunday School class right away. I'm not even waiting till Sunday; I'll start the prayer chain today."

"But everyone is preoccupied with the pastoral search," Marjorie hesitated. "I know that's important. Our church is in a real crisis. I don't think we can ask them to take on my problem too."

Catherine's reply was firm. "Nonsense," she declared. "We don't call ourselves Daniel's Dozen for nothing. This class prays, and we're going to pray for *you!*"

The Sunday School has an intercessory function. Because the leaders feel called to minister, they pray for their own work and for the work of the church. And within the intimate fellowship of the Sunday School classes, students pray for one another.

The Seedbed of Miracles

Some of the greatest answers to prayer have their beginnings in a Sunday School classroom. Don't look for millions of dollars or miraculous healings (although these have come about as answers to prayers launched in Sunday School). Look at all the lost pupils who have accepted Christ because a teacher or class has prayed for them.

There have been other great answers to prayer. Think of those called into full-time Christian service. Think of lonely people who have found a friend. Think of those aimless people who have found their spiritual gift and ended up in happy, meaningful service.

Miracles are possible through the corporate prayer of a Sunday School class or a small group. Jesus said, "Again I say to you that if two of you agree on earth concerning anything that they ask, it will be done for them by My Father in heaven" (Matt. 18:19). Why not bring the needs of the local church before one such group? Maybe you as a pastor can get great answers to prayer by having a Sunday School class pray for your needs. Must we be reminded that prayer was a great dynamic for the New Testament church? "And when they had prayed, the place where they were assembled together was shaken; and they were all filled with the Holy Spirit, and they spoke the word of God with boldness" (Acts 4:31).

Action Point: What is the spiritual temperature of prayer in your Sunday School?

The Beginnings of Prayer Ministry

In the New Testament, these bold believers were probably meeting in a house church in Jerusalem when the house was shaken. Today, that "place where they were assembling" could very well be a Sunday School classroom. Some church-shaking answers to prayer may well come out of that junior high classroom. Most of the time, activities coming out of a junior high classroom are measurable on the Richter Scale anyway—so why not use that group dynamic in intercessory prayer?

Don't limit intercessory prayer to the junior high department, though. There are some other exciting possibilities. Here are some great ways to enhance the prayer ministry of your church through Sunday School.

- *Use the 50-50 plan.* Insist that leaders allow 50 percent of their class time for group interaction, fellowship and prayer. (The other half of the class is for life-changing Bible study.)
- *Teach prayer.* The discipline and dynamics of intercession can be offered as an elective class. Students who know how to pray will be more apt to put those principles into action.
- *Pray with leaders.* Model the ministry of prayer by getting teachers and students to pray together before Sunday School starts.
- *Start an intercessors' class.* Some of your church folk feel called to a ministry of prayer. Find a time and place for them to meet for prayer. By doing so, you validate their calling and keep them praying.

- *Request prayer from classes.* Ask the young adults to take on the burden of prayer for evangelism. Request that your junior high kids pray, especially for a missionary family.
- *Follow the example of the watchers.* The Metropolitan Baptist Tabernacle in London, England, had a group of intercessors who met to pray during each worship service at the church. They met in the basement, directly beneath the pulpit. They were called "Watchers" because they prayed during the sermon, which usually lasted about an hour. The name of their prayer group was suggested by Jesus who asked all of us, "Could you not watch one hour?" (Mark 14:37). This church became one of the most influential in the British Empire during the 1800s—and many think that this was primarily due to their intercessors.
- *Two-pray.* Take time in a worship service for people to divide into groups of two for prayer. This way everyone has an opportunity to pray and people are drawn together as they approach the throne with corporate and individual requests.
- *Digital Requests.* Use the computer and the Internet to communicate prayer requests and answers with the Sunday School class. This will help people remember to pray during the week, and it will also serve as a connection to the members who missed class on Sunday.
- *Celebrate victories.* When you have answers to prayer, broadcast the good news. Let everyone see that his or her prayers are powerful and effective.
- *Build a team of pastor's prayer partners.* One of the most important tasks a pastor can do in a church is to build a team of intercessors who will pray specifically for him. The pastor should meet with them to share burdens

and requests. (See *Prayer Partners* by Elmer Towns; note chapter 9: "How to Find Prayer Partners," Regal Books, 2002.)

We often use prayer like aspirin. We only open the bottle when we have a migraine. But medical science tells us that aspirin has a preventive use as well. It can prevent clotting and enhance blood flow—resulting in longer and healthier life. If that's true in medicine, then we should look for the parallel in ministry: Prayer brings power and life to the local church ministry—and helps to prevent conflicts among the church family.

> **There's value in the volume of prayer.**
>
> JOHN ARNOLD

James the apostle knew the power of prayer: "Confess your trespasses to one another, and pray for one another. . . . The effective, fervent prayer of a righteous man avails much" (Jas. 5:16). The command to "pray for each other" may be one of the second most-neglected commissions given to the Church.

Sunday School is one place to make amends for that "Great Omission." The advantages of meeting in a smaller group setting certainly give your church members greater courage to pray—even pray out loud. The saying We're among friends reflects the breaking down of barriers, thus allowing for greater communication.

Action Point: What can you do to increase the amount of prayer in your church?

The Fuel of Faith

Releasing people to pray is a gigantic opportunity for ministry. Denny Gunderson said, "The awe-inspiring greatness of Christ's splendor is defined not by the power of his natural attributes, but by the unfathomable depth of character he exhibited in entrusting the developing and equipping of his Church into the hands of mortal leaders."[1]

Prayer is the fuel that powers a church. Sunday School is a laboratory that produces this powerful fuel. You have a Sunday School, so now focus on developing powerful, dedicated prayer warriors.

We all agree that prayer is a wonderful tool in the work of God, but sometimes, with everything we have on our plates, it's easy to let prayer slip. It's human. Look at Moses leading over a million people through the desert; he got tired too. When the Amalakites attacked, Joshua took the men to fight off the attackers, and Moses went into the mountain to pray. "And so it was, when Moses held up his hand, that Israel prevailed; and when he let down his hand, Amalek prevailed" (Exod. 17:11).

You probably want to pray and feel the need to pray for your church ministry. But like Moses, you run out of strength. What you need are some people like Aaron and Hur to hold you up in intercession. "But Moses' hands became heavy; so they took a stone and put it under him, and he sat on it. And Aaron and Hur supported his hands, one on one side, and the other on the other side; and his hands were steady until the going down of the sun" (Exod. 17:12).

▼

You've got fellow workers in your Sunday School—pray for them, then get them to pray with you. They'll hold up your hands in intercession!

Action Point: What can you do to recruit a group of intercessors who will be pastoral prayer partners?

Chapter 10

SUNDAY SCHOOL
WILL PROVIDE
TEACHING
EVANGELISM

"By the way, I've decided to become a follower of Jesus Christ," Tom Bradley told his pastor, as they shook hands at the front door of the church one Sunday after morning worship.

Pastor Greg McClain thought the decision had come as a result of his preaching. Tom Bradley had been attending Calvary Church for more than a year, and the pastor knew Tom wasn't saved because of a conversation they had had when Tom first started attending church. Tom had even gone through the new members' class taught by the pastor during Sunday School. But after the class was over, Tom was still not spiritually ready for membership. And so Pastor Greg had continued to pray for Tom's salvation.

"That's great," the pastor responded to the good news. "What motivated you to finally become a Christian?"

"It was your Sunday School class," Tom explained. "As we studied the lesson on becoming born again, I began to see Jesus in a new way. I had always thought of Jesus as a good teacher. Before that Sunday School class, I identified with Nicodemus when he complimented Jesus for being a good teacher. But when I learned that Jesus told Nicodemus in John 3:7, 'You must be born again,' I realized that I had not really trusted Him with my whole life. I suddenly knew that I needed to be born again."

Pastor Greg blinked. "Wow." The pastor had thought it was his sermon, but it was his teaching that had gotten through to Tom.

"Yeah," Tom continued, "I really got a lot out of your Sunday School class."

There are many who can be reached for salvation through teaching, rather than preaching. There are many who are dominated with rational thoughts, rather than influenced primarily by their emotions. They need *explanations*, rather than *motivations*. When their questions are answered and they see the reasons why they should be born again, they will trust Christ to forgive their sins.

Action Point: Examine your preaching. Do you give more explanation or more motivation when you preach? Both are needed, but perhaps you need Sunday School teachers who will present the gospel in a discussion setting, making your church well-rounded in its evangelistic outreach.

Answering Life Questions

The Sunday School is positioned to answer the questions of life that many in your church have.

People haven't found lasting answers in the textbooks of their times. Seekers across ecclesiastical and cultural lines are crowding together into living rooms, classrooms, lunchrooms, and online chat rooms in a quest to know more about where planet Earth came from, how they arrived on it, and where they will be going when they leave it. It's an opportune time for the Church to guide them to the eternal truths of God's Word![1]

Sometimes a sermon can't reach certain persons. They won't accept what is preached until their questions are answered. It's not that they are opposed to the gospel or to what is preached; it's just they can't put their faith in anything until their questions are answered. Their questions are like the hair and dirt that block the drain in the plumbing of a sink. The water can't drain freely until the blockage is removed. In the same way, these folks can't respond to the gospel until their questions are answered, until you give them reasons to believe and chances to discuss.

> *Teaching evangelism is the presentation of the gospel through the explanation of Scripture.*

People usually don't have an opportunity to ask their questions during a worship service. But a Sunday School class is different. Not only are they given freedom to ask questions about the things that "bug" them, but they are also encouraged to get into the discussion.

Although many kinds of evangelism can be effective—soul winning, preaching, crusades and gospel tracts—Sunday School may be best suited to *teaching evangelism*, the presentation of the gospel through the explanation of Scripture. In past years, Sunday School has been the primary instrument of the Church for bringing many to Christ. Teaching evangelism is as relevant as today's newspapers and magazines yet as old as the first-century church. Notice what happened in the Jerusalem church, "And they continued steadfastly in the apostles' doctrine [teaching] and fellowship, in the breaking of bread, and in prayers" (Acts 2:42). What was the result? "The Lord added to the church daily those who were being saved" (Acts 2:47). Teaching God's Word was central to the evangelistic ministry of the New Testament church.

Action Point: Do you provide an opportunity for people in your church to freely ask the questions that "bug" them?

Discovering the Word

Teaching evangelism is especially effective because it always provides a clear scriptural basis for salvation, so that every convert has a sound basis for his or her decision. "So then faith comes by hearing, and hearing by the word of God" (Rom. 10:17). Converts won by teaching evangelism are more likely to remain as active members of the church. What's more, they've already begun the process of discipleship.

Your Sunday School can be an evangelistic arm of your ministry. Here's how:

1. *Make evangelism a priority.* Be proactive about fulfilling the Great Commission through your church's program. Make sure that everyone involved in your ministry knows that evangelism isn't an add-on—it's the core. Discipleship without evangelism is like a coffee cup without coffee. The cup may be ceramic or crystal, antique or contemporary—but it's still a shell without its intended contents.

2. *Be sure every teacher understands how to present the gospel.* The assumption that your staff knows how to share

the gospel is a great *presumption*! Many times there is no presentation of the gospel because the teaching staff hasn't been trained in presenting it. When they are trained, they'll feel more confident. And besides, the training itself is your opportunity to make sure you've shared the plan of salvation with each teacher.

3. *Always point out the gospel story in each lesson.* It's there, from Genesis to Revelation. In your own teaching ministry, emphasize the story of saving grace in any text that you may present. Pointing out the signposts on the gospel road gives fellow travelers—as well as fellow guides—an important point of reference. Train your teaching staff to include an evangelistic appeal in their lessons.

4. *Designate Invitation Days.* Pick one day each month, each quarter or at least every year when an invitation to salvation will be given in every class. Promote Invitation Day in your church publications. Announce the opportunity enthusiastically from the pulpit. Make Invitation Day a special day. It is, in fact, one of the most important days in your church calendar year.

5. *Make plans to follow up on new converts.* Keep a record of those who make decisions, and then follow up those decisions with a new converts' class or new members' class. Whether leading children, adults or seniors, follow-up teaching is important to turning *deciders* into *disciples*. Use a decision card. The collection, care and keeping of those cards are extremely important!

There are prospects for evangelism in your Sunday School right now. More of them attend your worship service. How can you convert those seekers to believers? Initiate the practice of teaching evangelism in your Sunday School.

Action Point: Make a list of those things that can be done to make teaching evangelism more effective in your church. Discuss the points at staff meetings and then implement them.

Chapter 11

Sunday School Will Provide Instant Follow-Up for New Converts

The board of Christian education was stymied. "We just don't have enough workers to begin a new follow-up program of discipleship," protested Rita Thornton, the one member who always thought the cup was half empty. She could be relied upon to see the problems in everything.

"And I can't take on one more project," Ryan Adams chimed in. "We agree with you, Pastor, that we need a follow-up plan for new converts—but we just can't do it now."

Ridgeview Church was enjoying its best growth in more than 20 years, but it came at a cost. The church had added more than 40 people in worship attendance, about half of whom were new converts. A discipleship program aimed at teaching new converts was desperately needed, but the question was, who would staff it?

Pastor Jim Bush tried a different approach.

"Suppose we *did* start a new discipleship program. What would it look like?"

"Well," Rita began, "it would probably take a couple of classes to get the people involved—perhaps a meeting that ran for several weeks."

"And we'd need a curriculum of some kind," Ryan added. "And some trained leaders." Ryan thought a minute and then added, "Maybe a director, someone to oversee the whole thing?"

Not to be outdone, Rita added, "And you'd need some mature believers in the mix who could mentor or coach new believers—something like that."

"So let me get this straight," said Pastor Jim. "We need a series of study groups that meet for about an hour each week for Bible study, fellowship and accountability, staffed by trained leaders and including a broad mix of mature believers?"

You could see the lights come on. Rita and Ryan said simultaneously, "Sunday School!"

"Right," said Pastor Jim. "So what's next on the agenda?"

The Oldest and Best

Every church must have a follow-up program for new converts. Worship alone will not bring believers to maturity. The church needs a more purposeful program of teaching, fellowship and accountability.

Enter Sunday School. The Bible-teaching arm of the church is an outstanding place to ground new believers in the essentials of the faith.

This oldest of church ministries—over 200 years old—has always been aimed at discipleship. In one study of over 500

Protestant pastors, over 96 percent said that their church ministry offered systematic Bible study in a classroom setting—they were talking about Sunday School.

With an organized curriculum, Sunday School meets the internal needs of the new convert. Follow-up should not be a hit-and-miss, randomly thrown-together approach to building new babes in Christ into mature believers in Christ. Follow-up shouldn't just answer the questions that come off the top of the heads of new converts, although their questions do need to be answered. Follow-up must be an organized approach that works toward the goal of maturity and includes sequential study of the Word, with application to the needs of the young believer. Your follow-up classes must follow an agenda because there is an agenda built into each human.

> Spiritual development is not something mysterious. It does not occur without direction. There is a path and pattern. It occurs in a human life context, following an agenda structured by God. It involves the whole person. God has ordained an unfolding life pattern, some of it unique, some of it similar, in each of His children.[1]

Action Point: Where in your church is an organized, biblical approach that takes new believers in sequential steps toward maturity?

Disciple Making

Designing a part of the church's program specifically for new converts is simple.

Start a new converts' class.
Special classes for new converts should be created regularly. New believers will feel more comfortable in a class where everybody's a beginner. Choose a curriculum that is

geared specifically to new believers. Set a time limit for the course—six to eight weeks usually is best. Select a classroom (preferably a neat, visitor-friendly one—complete with a coffeepot). Advertise the class from the pulpit and in your church publications. Some will not want to attend a *new converts' class*, thinking they have been a Christian since birth. So call it the *new members' class* or *seekers' class*.

Announce the purpose.
Let people know that Sunday School isn't just for mature Christians or the core group. Sunday School is the best place for newcomers. It is a friendly place where people who want to be more like Christ can receive on-site instruction. Be sure everyone knows it. New converts' training purposefully tears down the portable classroom dividers between *us* and *them*. It's a seeker-friendly environment for new people in the church.

Train the staff.
Staffing is important in creating an effective new converts' class. If the pastor or other paid ministerial staff are not available, then a layperson with equally solid credentials should be appointed. The teacher of the new converts' class should definitely be someone who has a Barnabas personality—one who knows how to encourage as well as instruct new believers. The care and feeding of new converts can sometimes be tumultuous. Staff must be aware of the emotional and spiritual ups and downs of people new in their faith.

Make the referral.
As pastor, you'll be aware of new converts before most other ministry leaders. Direct them to a good Sunday

School class. When you have the privilege of winning a soul to Christ, immediately invite him or her to Sunday School—preferably to a class designed especially for new members. Your influence is vital. If you are enthusiastic about the basic training of new converts, it will result in an effective and long-term discipleship ministry.

▼ ─────────────────────────────────────

Do you have a follow-up program for new converts? If you have a Sunday School, the answer is yes. With a little bit of reinventing, you can turn Sunday-morning study time into a *discovery* time. Your attendees will not only be added to the church rolls, they will also be enlisted in a great campaign for souls. The new converts' class is only the beginning!

Action Point: What do you need to do to better use your Sunday School for discipleship purposes?

Chapter 12

SUNDAY SCHOOL WILL PROVIDE A FRIENDSHIP NETWORK

"Thursday's no good, Sarah. We're having some people over for dessert."

"What about next Saturday?"

"That's out too. We've been invited to a barbecue."

"OK, let's go for next month. How about the 19th?"

"Let me see . . . nope, we're hosting a birthday party for the Gonzales family. Hector's on temporary duty in Korea, so we're going to give his wife Carmen a hand with the kids."

Sarah tried to hide her disappointment. She'd been trying to get better acquainted with Jim and Leigh Rawlings, but there never seemed to be a good time. Jim and Leigh both were outgoing and seemed to have the gift of hospitality. They used gatherings at their home as a way to show the love of Christ to others. Finally,

Sarah, in a wistful voice, said, "Leigh, I can't believe you have so many friends." Sarah was half amazed and half envious.

Leigh answered the question with another question, "Why don't you and Ron come over on Thursday evening? We've wanted to get together with you guys, and this would be a perfect opportunity. All your friends will be there."

"All *my* friends?" Sarah was puzzled. "I would be out of place with your friends—I wouldn't know a soul."

"Sure you would," Leigh responded. "They're all people from church—the Greens, the Bentons, Phil and Joanne Lyon, Carmen Gonzales—you know all of them."

"I guess so," Sarah paused. "I just didn't realize you were all friends."

"Well of course," said Leigh. "We're all in the same Sunday School class."

Sunday School provides the glue that bonds people to your church. And what is that glue? It's the relationship that members have with one another. When they become a part of each other's lives, they find a place to belong. Like glue, they stick together and become friends.

Action Point: *How do you promote friendship among the members of your church?*

Need for Friendships

Worship services attract people to the church; Sunday School keeps them. Sunday School provides a network of small groups in which people form relationships with one another. They become bonded to the church.

Newcomers especially are hungry for relationships. A quick handshake in the pew during a praise chorus just isn't enough. In this fast and furious world, people need more than a passing wave—they need spiritual fellowship. Having recently moved, come to know Christ or changed churches, they've broken old relationships and are looking to form new ones.

In a mobile culture in which many people are looking for connections, Sunday School is the perfect setting for forging new friendships. Those who join a class will likely form friendships within weeks, and such friendships will fill a growing need in our culture. Rabey comments:

> Over the past twenty centuries, older ideas about community have been challenged by newer concepts of the autonomy of the individual. Although a commitment to the dignity of every person is an idea with plentiful biblical support, there is growing evidence that our single-minded commitment to individualism has robbed us of the joys of community.[1]

Someone once said, "Sunday School is the church doing its work. Sunday School does not have tasks or work to do apart from the work that belongs to the church." So Sunday School isn't a part of the church—it is the church! Yes, getting visitors into the church ministry is the goal, but Sunday School is how you keep them there.

Action Point: How big is the problem of isolation in your church? What types of small groups do you have at your church that foster fellowship and the growth of friendships?

Sunday School Networking

Every church is a massive network—like a giant spiderweb—with each section attached to another. Nothing remains in the network without being connected to another. If each individual remains alone, he or she is like a single spider's thread. But when attached together, the threads become a web. A church of isolated individuals is nothing more than spectators at a religious gathering. The church only truly becomes a church when each person becomes attached to all others through shared relationships. Here are some things to help Sunday School networking.

1. *Sunday School groups people with shared needs.* Age grouping—the most common arrangement for Sunday School classes—gathers together people with shared lifestyles. People meeting in age groups are on the same level. They not only feel more comfortable in their group, they are also more apt to form relationships with their group members—and consequently are more apt to form a relationship with the local church ministry. Sunday School is a "gospel glue."

2. *Sunday School builds intimacy.* People get to know each other in Sunday School. By sharing prayer requests, discussing issues and working on projects together, they become well acquainted. Social relationships form quickly in a small group. Sunday School is a perfect antidote for the loneliness that plagues our twenty-first-century society.

3. *Sunday School provides an excuse for socializing.* People love to get together, and Sunday School is the perfect excuse. Encourage classes to bring donuts or organize potluck dinners, picnics, pool parties and cookouts.

4. *Sunday School is the quickest point of connection.* Newcomers who do not join a Sunday School class may take months to form relationships in the church—if they do so at all. Many will be lost to the church because they do not find a home within the larger congregation. Sunday School is a quick connect for relationship building, as new members of the church find their place in the Body of Christ.

We must in every way, become more and more like Jesus who is the head of the body. We are members of one another and of Him. He works through His Body to fit each of us together, perfectly joined at the right place, at the right time, to do the right thing. Each of us in the Body does our part, and we help each of the others in the Body to become mature in the faith. When we all fit into our place in the Body, the church becomes healthier, and each individual in the church grows to become like Jesus Christ (Eph. 4:15-16, author's translation).

Sunday School and small-group relationships bond people to the ministry of the local church—the Body. They fill a social need as well as a ministry need. In an age of gated communities, the church offers an open door. In a culture of doormen and high-rise apartments, the church invites people into the fellowship hall for coffee. In a world of retina-scan identification, the church extends the right hand of fellowship to all.

When Jesus said, "Come to Me"(Matt. 11:28), He meant every person. So two people who come to Jesus find themselves one in Jesus (see John 17:20-26). They have a basis for relationship and friendship. Nearly every newcomer to your congregation needs more than a place to worship. He or she needs friendship with other Christians. Loneliness is the problem. Sunday School is the solution.

Action Point: How can you make your Sunday School more receptive to relationships and friendships?

Chapter 13

SUNDAY SCHOOL WILL PROVIDE LIFE COACHING

"David, can I talk with you for a minute?"

"Of course, Jeff. What's up?"

"A couple of weeks ago you requested prayer about your job. I wanted to see if things were going any better." Jeff was an older Christian who had been in the church all his life. He was level-headed, and the men of the church looked up to him. Jeff was also spiritual. He knew the Scriptures and how to apply them to life; but more important, Jeff knew God personally and could pray effectively. That's why Dave had come to him with his concerns in the first place.

David Barnett had been under a good deal of stress and it showed. His company was being acquired by a multinational holding company, and the change in management was wreaking havoc on employee morale. Dave explained to Jeff, "Actually, my problem is worse. Scam Corp announced last week that they're cutting another 50 jobs. I had to lay off three of my best engineers."

"That must have been tough."

"But that's not the worst of it. The new management has no idea how our business works. They're making some bad moves—we've lost two of our best accounts. After 22 years with this company, I'm ready to walk out the door."

"Can you afford that?" Jeff asked, hoping Dave wasn't planning to make a foolhardy decision.

"No, but I can't live like this either. The stress is killing me. Jeannie feels it too. I'm just not sure what to do."

"You know, I went through something like that when I sold my construction business. It was the toughest choice I ever made. I'd be glad to talk you through your options sometime."

"That'd be great. I really need some help sorting out this decision. Maybe we could have lunch this week."

"Sure, Dave. I'll give you a call."

Mentors and Coaches

No one person has all the answers. Each Christian depends on others for insight, advice and help in solving problems. "Life coaching" is a growing phenomenon that's fast becoming a cottage industry. But Sunday School offers the same service without charge! Sunday School provides a network of experienced believers who serve as mentors, or coaches, to others. And these coaches are often more helpful than pastors or professional counselors because they come from the same world as the folks they help. These coaches have faced similar problems and can share their wisdom. The New Testament church had that same kind of mentoring network:

Now all who believed were together, and had all things
in common, and sold their possessions and goods, and
divided them among all, as anyone had need. So continuing daily with one accord in the temple, and breaking
bread from house to house, they ate their food with
gladness and simplicity of heart (Acts 2:44-46).

Sunday School is just such a New Testament, supportive
kind of place. In its friendly and faithful environment, people
receive life-changing advice and encouragement from other
members. In most churches, in a Sunday School room of 10 or
12 adults, there is a bank of experience and a web of influence
that is almost priceless. What do you need? Investment advice?
There's Joe the CFA. Parenting principles? Milly and Ralph
recently graduated from adolescent university! Automotive
expertise? Edward is a full-time middle school teacher and a
part-time mechanic. Plumbing problems? Every do-it-yourselfer
in the class knows about Chris the plumber's expertise in fixing
toilets. Need a stock tip? Angie is a broker with character!

The Small-Group Possibilities

Usually knowledge, experience and generosity all exist in any
given church body. But it's hard to find what, or rather who, you
need when you sit in a large crowd of people called a church
congregation. Worship is a possible site, when you shake hands
for two minutes, but there's not usually a lot of talk about
carburetors during the Sunday-morning service! A small group
is the better environment. No, a small setting is where you learn
about others and their strengths. Sunday School is just such a
place: a small group that serves as a great place to network.

Just think about all the possible ways in which your Sunday
School could provide mentoring to believers.

Spiritual accountability. All believers need accountability. Sunday School provides a place for mature believers to partner with younger ones, holding them accountable to resist temptation, keep their commitments and continue growing in the Spirit. This is especially important in the children and young-adult Sunday School classes, as these ages are highly impressionable. Provide stable Christians to teach and walk with children because they need accountability as they mature in their faith.

Life decisions. Choosing a college. Getting married. Buying a house. Changing careers. In every congregation, someone is in the process of making a decision about one of those things. If that person is a member of a Sunday School class, he or she will be surrounded by experienced mentors.

Call to ministry. How do I know if I'm called to ministry? The person who participates in a Sunday School class can discover the answer easier than the Christian without trusted friends.

Spiritual growth. Every Christian should continually grow in the Spirit. But it's not always easy. Believers face temptations and tough choices. Sunday School teachers and experienced leaders help others rise above those temptations and make the right choices.

Action Points: Make a list of all the life decisions, issues and problems that your members face. In what areas can you help? In those areas where you can't, who can your members seek out for guidance?

The Lay-Leader Benefits

The influence of fellow laypersons is invaluable to Christians seeking to grow in their faith. Williams and Gangel got it right:

Effective local church programs have always been lay led. When churches buy into the super professionalism of

modern society, they may design slick platform opera-
tions and in the process lose the interest of people who
desperately need to be involved and whose spiritual gifts
can contribute significantly to the overall ministry of
the congregation.[1]

Putting experienced leaders "in their place" is one of the keys
to church growth. Their place is in leading people—in sharing
life skills that will be a great benefit to the overall congregation.
Sunday School is an ideal setting. Nonthreatening interaction
happens there almost 52 weeks out of the year (except for
Christmas-program Sunday and the Easter pageant!).

▼
_____

Life coaching is a service for which many people are willing to
pay. You can give it away for free—if you have a Sunday
School.

*Action Point: How can you use the pulpit to encourage your
congregation to take advantage of the life coaching found in Sunday
School classes?*

Chapter 14

SUNDAY SCHOOL WILL TEACH CHURCHMANSHIP

"Nine dollars and 47 cents? That's all?" The new pastor was shocked when he heard the sum total of the funds in the church's bank account.

"Yep, I'm afraid so, Pastor. That's the balance in our general fund," the church treasurer answered.

Pastor John Byers didn't know whether to be amused or infuriated. When he'd accepted the call to Fall Creek Church, he knew that the church had some problems, but he hadn't expected the closing balance on the first month's financial report to be this low. "And you say there's another problem?" John asked.

"Yep," Freda Anders, the church treasurer, continued. "Regina Zimmerman resigned today."

"Regina Zimmerman?"

"Yep. She was the director of volunteer ministries."

"Was there a problem?"

"Yep. She couldn't get any volunteers."

Pastor John expressed his frustration to Freda: "There's no money coming in, no one will volunteer to staff the nursery, and there are two vacancies on the church board that haven't been filled in over two years. Yet we have more than 100 people in attendance at church every Sunday. Is that right?"

"Yep."

"When I interviewed here, you told me that fewer than 10 years ago, you had a surplus of $10,000 in the general fund and a waiting list for the leadership committee, even though there were fewer than 60 people in church every week."

"Yep."

"So what happened?" Pastor Byers's question had a tinge of sadness. "Why were things in such good shape 10 years ago but not now? Can you think of any reason why things fell apart?"

"Yep," Freda said flatly. "Ten years ago we had Sunday School."

What Freda was saying was that Sunday School gave the church infrastructure. When a church has an operative Sunday School, it's more than likely that all members will use their spiritual gifts. When everyone is using his or her gifts in service to the church, all the necessary tasks are fulfilled and thus all of the church's goals are realized.

Action Point: Play the game "What If." Ask yourself and the staff, "What if our church didn't have a Sunday School?"

Realizing the Investment

People are not naturally inclined toward commitment. In fact, they avoid making commitments to just about anything. Modern Americans are skeptical of institutions and don't want to get involved. It may be that they are busier than ever, but also it's the spirit of the times: Stay free; leave your options open; let someone else do it. One result is that people are not as loyal to their church as they used to be. Many people love their church and enjoy attending worship services, but they do not realize the personal investment of time and money that's needed to keep any volunteer organization going—especially the church.

Sunday School can reverse this trend. Sunday School teaches churchmanship to secular-minded North Americans. When you teach churchmanship, you tap into the great potential for making *contributing members* out of *regular attendees*.

Abstract Christianity becomes real Christianity in a smaller group setting. In a classroom setting, showing financial giving charts and collecting offerings naturally lead to prayer requests. The needs of the church don't change, but the urgency is personalized during the small-group discussion. It's no longer *their* problem; it's now *our* problem. Numbers crunched in a finance committee meeting take on a new meaning when they're involved with buying what you need to do your church ministry.

> *Churchmanship is every member loving his or her church, serving through the church, advancing the purposes of the church and worshiping the Lord in the church; it is making the church work for the glory of God.*

The infrastructure of a church concerns much more than the way an organization is managed. The church is a body (see Eph. 1:22-23). Members are asked to do more than *volunteer*. They are asked to be loyal to Jesus Christ. When they serve their church, they are serving the Body of Jesus Christ. And when members refuse to get involved with His Body, ask yourself a question, Are they involved with Christ?

Further, churchmanship is not grudging involvement. The Bible says, "Christ also loved the church and gave Himself for her" (Eph. 5:25). So members must love their church with the same love that Jesus had. That's a high standard, and not many members meet it.

Churchmanship, however, should not be confined to the adult members of your church. Children can learn to be involved and committed to their Sunday School classes if they are taught correctly at a young age. This lesson of churchmanship will shape them into adult church members with integrity.

So use the Sunday School to build churchmanship into your worshipers. First, make sure the Sunday School teaches churchmanship; then get all members involved. Lastly, use your preaching to support the church's need for more involved churchmanship, the need for everyone to get involved. Work with your Sunday School, so it can work with you.

Action Point: Have you really thought about churchmanship as the viable involvement of every church worshiper? Could Sunday School help you get regular attendees to be more active in the life of the church?

Providing Solutions through Churchmanship

Sunday School encourages churchmanship, and churchmanship requires dedication to the Body. With this kind of commitment, members will do everything possible to solve the problems they face and keep the Body healthy.

Problem solving more often begins at the small-group level than with the sanctuary crowd. A class can often get a handle on a solution for a church problem more easily than the corporate assembly. Ideas that float freely around a small group would be stifled or overlooked in a larger meeting.

Sunday School is a place where a believer's responsibility to his or her church is taught firsthand. Here are some valuable lessons you can teach in your Sunday School:

Tithing.
Pastors are sometimes reluctant to speak directly about church finances. Sunday School teachers aren't. Why? Because they are usually tithers themselves. A message on stewardship coming from a fellow layperson is easier to digest than one coming from the vocational ministry staff.

Volunteerism.
In Sunday School, everybody pitches in. The small-group setting leaves no place for the slacker to hide. In a growing church, people can easily become pew warmers—faces in the crowd. But in a small-group setting, people *do* more because more is expected of them. They are closer to the need, and they see their friends pitch in. For example, a sanctuary announcement about the need for volunteers to stack chairs in the fellowship hall may be ignored by most. But the same listener in a fellowship hall *classroom* has more difficulty ignoring the stacking announcement because he's been sitting on one of the chairs. Peer pressure is involved. People learn to *load their share* by *sharing the load.*

Church loyalty.
Sunday School provides more in-depth teaching about the church than any other agency in the church. It's here that local church distinctives are taught—and valued. A quarterly teaching on the beliefs of the local church not

only helps to ground members spiritually, it also con-
tributes to their "brand loyalty." Questions and answers
that wouldn't be appropriate in a sanctuary worship setting may be handled easily in a Sunday School classroom. And when people have questions regarding why
the church does the things it does, those questions can
be answered in a class
setting; whereas there is
no place to ask the ques-
tion in a worship service.
Especially in an age of
corporate capers and big-
business misgivings, peo-
ple want up-front answers about the organizations they
join. Sunday School is a good place to answer the questions inquiring minds need to know.

> *Ask not what my church can do for me, Ask what can I do for my church.*

Big-picture thinking.
The people who attend the large worship gatherings
have the smallest view—they see only what the church
does for them. Those who attend the smaller gathering
have a larger view—they see what they can do for the
church. Worship is often an arena sport in which folks
sit in the stands, waiting for the next spine-tingling
musical, dramatic or oratorical rendition; whereas the
Sunday School or small-group setting gets people
involved in the trenches, serving the Lord and making
the local church happen.

I s your church mired in "me-ism"? A revitalized Sunday School ministry is one important solution. It shows people the cost of church in time, energy and finances. It lets members offer solutions to complex church problems. And it helps them to support and get involved in what they have up to now only enjoyed.

Action Point: How can you utilize your Sunday School to teach churchmanship, i.e., the involvement of every member?

Chapter 15

Sunday School Will Make Use of All Spiritual Gifts

"Greg?"

The teacher of the Life Connection class was shocked that his pastor would suggest Greg Wilson as a class worker. The teacher rephrased his skepticism, "You're giving me Greg as an assistant for my Sunday School class?"

"Sure," Pastor Rick Rasberry answered. "You said that you need help with the Life Connection class. And Greg's available."

Pastor Rick can't be serious, thought Cameron. Cam Secord was an energetic sales agent for a high-tech firm. When he and his wife, Tammy, took over the leadership of the young-adult class, it instantly attracted a group of sharp young professionals. They renamed the class Life Connection, designed a hot logo and started a web page. Cam and Tammy thought of it as the "in" place at Westwood Community Church.

Suddenly Cameron blurted out, "It's just that Greg . . . well, Greg's—" Cam didn't know how to phrase his concern, so the pastor did it for him.

"A geek?"

"I was going to say dork," Cameron replied. "But, yeah, Greg's just not Life Connection material."

The pastor drew a long breath—it was time to play senior pastor. "Cameron, do you know what Greg does for a living?"

"I'd say he's an accountant, judging by the way he dresses—he always has that bow tie perfectly straight."

"You're right," the pastor quickly replied. "Greg's an accountant. He happens to be an accounting manager—the CFO for Bowes and McKinney, to be exact. Greg keeps track of a little more than a half billion dollars per year, and he pulls down a salary probably bigger than anyone in the class."

"Oh."

"And didn't you tell me you needed help in the Life Connection class?"

"I need organization," Cam, the supersalesman, said. "I've got all these people coming, but I can't keep track of who's there and who has a prayer need. We can't get any events planned. There's a lot of energy, but I need someone to give some structure to it."

"So you need an administrator, someone to keep up with the details?" the pastor asked.

"Right."

"If Greg has the ability to keep track of millions of dollars at work, don't you think God could use his gift in the church?"

"I guess so." Cam looked uncomfortable. "But what about his wife?"

"Dora? What about her?"

"Nobody likes her, that's what. She doesn't say much, but when she does, it's always negative."

"Let me tell you something about Dora. Last year when we hired a youth pastor, Dora was on the search committee. She voted against the first candidate, practically torpedoed his nomination single-handedly, without a good reason."

"That doesn't surprise me."

"It turned out that the fellow had some false statements on his resume. Nobody knew that at the time, but Dora's judgment was right. That's called discernment, and it's a gift of the Holy Spirit."

"Oh." Cam smiled sheepishly. "Alright, Pastor Rick. I'll call Greg and Dora this afternoon. Seems like I could use a little discernment, couldn't I?"

Every church should, theoretically, use everyone in ministry. That's God's plan, "The whole body ministering to the whole body" (Eph. 4:16, author's translation). But if everyone had the same ability (spiritual gift), then all would be clamoring to do the same job in the same way. But that's not God's plan. God has given different gifts to each person, different strengths to help him or her get the job done—we call this the *gift mix*, the unique combination of gifts within each person.

Action Point: Have you ever looked at people in your church by focusing on their gifts and the strength of each of those gifts? First, try sizing up your staff; then try sizing up the church board; finally, try to size up some of the gifted leaders in the church. Use these gifted people in your Sunday School classes.

Locating the Spiritual-Gift Shop

One key to success is using people according to their abilities. Every spiritual gift is necessary if the church is to operate effectively, and Sunday School is a place where each person can discover and use their spiritual gifts. It may take a little search and recovery, but it's there. Every gift needed to add power and pizzazz to your church ministry has already been stocked on the shelves of your constituents' hearts.

> For as we have many members in one body, but all the members do not have the same function, so we, being many, are one body in Christ, and individually members of one another. Having then gifts differing according to the grace that is given to us, let us use them: if prophecy, let us prophesy in proportion to our faith; or ministry, let us use it in our ministering; he who teaches, in teaching; he who exhorts, in exhortation; he who gives, with liberality; he who leads, with diligence; he who shows mercy, with cheerfulness (Rom. 12:4-8).

Action Point: Is your church tuned in to the spiritual-gift renaissance that is happening today? Have you preached on spiritual gifts lately? If you were to preach on gifts again, what would you expect to happen?

Opening the Gifts

Sunday School can be like Christmas every day, a place where you can help others open their spiritual gifts, the abilities that God has given to them. What can Sunday School do?

Sunday School Helps People Identify Their Gifts

People don't always know what their gifts are. The small-group environment of a Sunday School provides a place for affirmation and feedback in ministry. A 12-week, small-group study of spiritual gifts could be just the eye-opener someone needs: "Help . . . I can do that!" And the positive reaction of fellow class or group members could be just the affirmation that person needs to start a personal ministry. (For further reading, see the textbook, *Your Spiritual Gifts Can Make Your Church Grow* by C. Peter Wagner, Regal Books, 1994.)

Sunday School Provides a Place to Experiment with Ministry

Sunday School provides entry-level ministry. This is one of the first places most people put their spiritual gifts to work. It's a place to learn, succeed and grow. "As each one has received a gift, minister it to one another, as good stewards of the manifold grace of God" (1 Pet. 4:10). A teacher needs that fourth-grade class just as much as the class needs a teacher. The appointment could mean far more than "warm-body placement." It could mean the revitalization of the spiritual life of a dormant Christian.

Sunday School Provides a Place of Expression for Some Gifts

Worship services make use of prophets, exhorters and teachers. But what about those who aren't gifted in these areas? Where do they minister? Sunday School makes use of many gifts, including some that seldom find expression. Encouragers motivate others to be positive and practical. Helpers minister in serving tasks as publicity coordinators, assistants, treasurers, greeters, etc. Administrators are "slot" people; they put the right person in the right job, to do the right things, at the right time, for the right purpose. Mercy showers are the counselors who listen with empathy and sympathy, helping people solve their problems. Those with the gift of evangelism follow up with absentees, contact prospects and, of course, witness decisions. And don't forget those with the spiritual gift of giving; they give their time, talent and treasure to get the work of God done.

▼

Sunday School plays an essential role in helping your congregation be the best it can be by using *everyone's* spiritual gifts. Without this vital function, your church may be lacking an essential Body part!

Action Point: What percentage of people in your congregation have identified their spiritual gifts and are using them?

Chapter 16

SUNDAY SCHOOL WILL PROVIDE SPIRITUAL CARE

To my friends in the Couples' Class—

I can't thank you enough for the help you've given me over the past three years, especially these last few weeks. When Bert was diagnosed with Parkinson's, I was driven to despair. Frantic at the thought of losing my husband, I was also burdened immediately with the demands of his care. But I was not alone. You all supported us in many ways. Marjorie, I treasure the times you came to talk with me and help with Bert's care. And thank you, Fred; you were nearly a full-time taxi driver, taking Bert to the doctor and therapist. The cards, notes and phone calls of encouragement from all of you were deeply appreciated.

But there was another burden I carried, one that I told few of you about. I was stricken with anger and doubt. I was angry with God for not granting my requests for healing. And I was doubtful—at times on the verge of giving up faith altogether. Again, you were my support. Charlie's faithful teaching each week was a blessing to me. And, Louise, I know that I nearly talked your ear off. Thank you for listening, for understanding my anger and for giving me freedom to speak my mind.

Most of all, thank you all for being with me at the funeral home last week. I rejoice in knowing that Bert is with the Lord. I'm grateful to my friends in the Couples' Class for your caring, wisdom and patience.

Sincerely,

Margaret Foster

It is impossible for a pastor to give spiritual care to every person in a large congregation. Sunday School can be there for you—extending spiritual care in units of 10 or 20 people.

Benefits of Sunday School

Each person in the congregation can receive individualized spiritual attention from a Sunday School teacher and a network of mature believers.

Here are some benefits—both spiritual and practical—that Sunday School classes provide.

Crisis Ministry

When one member has an illness or family emergency, other class members rally support. Their very actions symbolize the community that has developed within this arm of the church ministry. The class becomes an extension of the vocational ministry staff. They are on-site representatives of the senior pastor and his or her pastoral staff. They also become their eyes and ears, as well as their heart. They can see firsthand what the need is and respond appropriately.

Spiritual Inquiry

Sunday School is a safe place to ask questions and voice concerns. Again, the community of the Sunday School class or small group affords a greater degree of intimacy than sanctuary worship. In a small group, feelings are expressed verbally—and non-verbally—that may be too personal for a corporate worship atmosphere. The camaraderie of the small group lends itself to openness, and openness is a great step toward spiritual healing.

> *The Sunday School teacher is a shepherd, extending the ministry of the senior pastor into the life of every person in a Sunday School class. Everything the senior pastor is and does can be delegated and carried out by each Sunday School teacher.*

Prayer Support

Sunday School supplies the primary prayer network for its members. Real needs become prayer requests for the group. And in a positive sense, that common knowledge of shared concerns is a bond that cements the group to the larger church. It is always a great encouragement to know that someone cares enough to pray about the things that burden you. In the context of the Sunday School, a teacher's caring support becomes a source of great spiritual strength. Jesus exemplified the principle, "But I have prayed for you, that your faith should

not fail; and when you have returned to Me, strengthen your
brethren" (Luke 22:32).

Encouragement

Class members often perceive the spiritual needs of their class-
mates and offer unsolicited encouragement or support in times
of need. Class members affirm one another. Those who have
been weakened by the week's events have sympathetic friends
who will give them a shoulder to lean upon and a hand to lift
them up. The Bible does not say in vain, "Bear one another's
burdens" (Gal. 6:2). Sunday School classes are also a great place
to celebrate victories. The affirmation that is scarce in the marketplace is common in a class or small group. Rejoicing with
those who rejoice is a characteristic of Christian community
that is best displayed in a small-group setting.

Tangible Help

Providing meals or transportation, lending a hand with yard
work, offering respite care or child care—these are commonplace
activities for a Sunday School class. The spirit of Dorcas is alive
in most Sunday Schools. "At Joppa there was a certain disciple
named Tabitha, which is translated Dorcas. This woman was full
of good works and charitable deeds which she did" (Acts 9:36).
Those lives that have been touched by the TLC of a Sunday
School class or small group are usually made stronger in their
allegiance to the parent-church body. "Therefore, as we have
opportunity, let us do good to all, especially to those who are of
the household of faith" (Gal. 6:10).

Teaching

Don't forget the obvious. Sunday School is a place where people
can grow spiritually from the study of God's Word. Vibrant Sunday
School classes are like a meeting of the New Testament Bereans.

"These were more fair-minded than those in Thessalonica, in that they received the word with all readiness, and searched the Scriptures daily to find out whether these things were so" (Acts 17:11).

As a pastor, you have more parishioner needs than you have hours in the day. Sunday School multiplies the spiritual care that your church can offer by multiplying the number of care-givers.

Action Point: What could happen if all teachers in your Sunday School saw themselves as an extension of your pastoral ministry?

The Biggest Little Church in the World!

I (Elmer) interviewed Pastor Yonggi Cho of the Yoido Full Gospel Church in Seoul, South Korea, when attendance at his church was averaging 170,000 per week. The church had 17,000 small groups meeting all over the city of Seoul in living rooms, meeting rooms of apartment buildings, plus recreation rooms, restaurants or any place a group of 10 to 12 adults could gather. The largest church in the world did its entire ministry to individuals—care giving, visiting absentees, problem counseling, visitation and prayer for the sick and prayer for one another—in the small groups. This church received the offerings from each member through its small groups, plus did its teaching, equipped future teachers and reached out in soul-winning evangelism. As of the writing of this book, the church has over 750,000 members with approximately 75,000 small groups. When I recently visited a Friday-night group of seven men in a Burger King restaurant booth, I felt their excitement of serving the Lord, plus their enthusiasm to study the Word. I stayed until I felt I was a damper on their excitement—they spoke Korean while I spoke only English. As I left them, I thought how powerful each church in America could be if their members were involved in a small-group Bible study as were these men.

▼ ──────────────────────────────────────

Spiritual care is at the core of every church's needs. It grows God's church while it draws people to the love of Jesus. And it is best actualized in small groups and Sunday School classes.

Action Point: Ask God to give you a vision to build a small-group ministry in your church and Sunday School.

Chapter 17

SUNDAY SCHOOL WILL
TEACH FAITHFULNESS

"I can't stand you, Traci. You're so—perfect!" Traci's friend was not putting her down nor was she criticizing. Traci's friend was giving her a compliment in a backhanded way.

Traci Abrams answered, "Don't be silly, Jill." Then she smiled. "Ron and I are just as normal as everyone else."

"I mean it," Jill Dayton persisted. "You're so together. Your whole life is under control. Jack and I are always struggling to pay bills, keep the car running and get the kids to behave. We can't even get to church on time!"

Traci laughed, but she understood her young friend's problem, so she explained, "Ron and I didn't always have it together." Traci continued her sympathetic counsel, "There was a time when we had real financial problems and nearly lost our house. Honestly, I didn't think our marriage was going to make it."

Jill was nonplussed. "You? I don't believe it."

"It's true," said Traci. "We spent every dime we made—and more. Ron's landscape business failed because we just weren't managing it well, and I . . . well, I nearly made a terrible mistake."

"But that's so unlike you both," Jill said with amazement. "You're the most disciplined people I know."

"We've grown a lot," Traci said thoughtfully. "It was around that time that Frank and Rita invited us to the Life Partners Sunday School class."

"Sunday School? I don't see how Sunday School could help us much. The last thing we need is one more meeting to attend—and one more deadline every week."

"There's where you're wrong, Jill. It was that 'one more deadline' that saved our home. It was the first building block of structure in our lives. Our Sunday School teachers, Frank and Rita, looked for us every Sunday, so we attended faithfully. When we skipped a Sunday, one of them would phone. Don't get me wrong, they never tried to give us a guilt trip for missing—they simply asked how they could pray for us."

"Wow!"

"Then Frank taught a series of lessons on household finances, and we started tithing. Giving God the first 10 percent forced us to discipline the rest of our finances."

Jill's eyes narrowed. "And what about your—temptation?"

"Oh, that," said Traci. "Let's just say that it's a little easier to be faithful when there are six other couples counting on you. Ron and I have never been happier."

Encouraging Self-Discipline

One of the challenges of the modern church is to teach faithfulness in daily living. A society that holds personal freedom as the ultimate value does not encourage people to honor their commitments. But Sunday School does! Its structured nature encourages

> *When you teach stewardship, you teach believers to properly manage their time, talent and treasure for the glory of God.*

self-discipline, promotes good stewardship and assists people in developing accountability.

The faithfulness of the church to its message and its mission is just as imperative as its vibrancy and influence. But it must also move beyond the structure of such objectives—into the daily lives of its adherents. It must move to help the fallen and strengthen the weakened in positive and tangible ways.

> The church must get another glimpse of the Savior praying on the hillside, "O Jerusalem, Jerusalem, you who kill the prophets and stone those sent to you, how often I have longed to gather your children together, as a hen gathers her chicks under her wings, but you were not willing" (Matt. 23:37). Today's church must hear the heartbeat of the One who was people-focused and purpose-driven in all of His earthly ministry.[1]

When you help someone become faithful, you strengthen him or her to build faithfulness in others.

Action Point: How faithful are the people in your congregation? How can you help Sunday School workers build faithfulness in others?

Strengthening Faithfulness

The Sunday School strengthens faithfulness in several ways.

Regular attendance. Many churches attempt to record members' attendance through sign-in sheets, roll books or other methods, but it's nearly impossible to keep up with everyone.

Attendees can drift in and out of the worship service for several weeks without being noticed. But Sunday School class members know almost immediately when someone is absent. That accountability helps promote more regular attendance.

Giving. People can contribute to their church through their Sunday School class offering. The smaller group setting creates a greater sense of responsibility among members. That feeling of responsibility spills over into other church giving as well. Even in childhood, the responsibility of giving to the Sunday School offering instills faithfulness to the church that can last lifelong.

Marriage. Sunday School classes become close-knit fellowships. Married couples find a strong support system for their marriages in Sunday School. They're all in it together, and together they can build strong marriages.

Ministry. Again, Sunday School classes offer a place to utilize spiritual gifts. The administration of the spiritual abilities that God has given helps the individual class members grow in faithfulness.

Prayer and Bible study. The Sunday School promotes faithfulness in the devotional life of its members. Testimonies of God's help in time of need, sharing of favorite Bible verses, witnessing to answers to prayer and helpful recommendations of devotional materials are among the incentives that lead to faithfulness. In the context of a Sunday School class or a small group, each feels accountable to one another (see Gal. 6:2) and accountability for themselves (see Gal. 6:5).

▼ ──────────────────────────────

What social force will counter the societal trend toward absolute freedom? Where is the place that young believers will develop discipline, learn accountability and become faithful members of their families, church and community? Sunday School.

Ezekiel's prophecy is a stirring clarion call to the church today. "So I sought for a man among them who would make a wall, and stand in the gap before Me on behalf of the land, that I should not destroy it; but I found no one" (Ezek. 22:30). Those who will bridge the gap can be found in Sunday School classes or small groups in your church.

Action Point: *What are the areas of faithfulness needed in your church? What activities can you or the Sunday School leaders encourage that will promote faithfulness?*

Chapter 18

Sunday School Will Build Character

"What's the big deal? It's not going to kill you. Besides, nobody will know." The whispered talk in the men's bathroom just told you something sinister was about to happen. The teenaged boys didn't want anyone else to hear them.

"I just don't feel like drinking it, that's all," a timid voice responded. The tone in his voice told you he was intimidated.

Trent and Adam had become friends on their first day at middle school band camp. Now, on their first night in the dorm, Adam wondered whether he knew Trent at all.

"That's because you've never tried it," Trent persisted, offering the soft drink container to Adam. "Besides, you won't even taste it. It's mixed with soda."

It was true that Adam had never tried alcohol. And he hated feeling like an outsider. Still, he didn't really want to drink. In Sunday School he had heard that it was a bad idea to start drinking alcohol.

"I'm telling you, nobody will know," Trent persisted.

Adam thought of what Andy Miller, the junior high boys' Sunday School teacher at New Hope Church, said: "Character is what you look like in the dark—character is what you do when nobody's looking."

Adam hesitated.

"What are you, chicken?" Trent then flapped his arms like a chicken, "Bok, bok, bok."

Adam could hear Andy's voice: "Character is what makes a man—a real man—a follower of Christ."

"No," Adam's voice stiffened, his eyes were determined. "I'm not a chicken. And I don't want to drink. That's something I just don't do."

Action Point: Evaluate Sunday School topics and curriculum to see how each subject might address temptation. Does each Sunday School class build character?

Key Quality: Character

Character is defined as habitually doing the right thing in the right way. People with convictions have character. They know who they are. They know what they believe. And they act accordingly.

From the towers of business to the halls of congress, character seems to be missing during these tumultuous times. The financial scandals of the age aren't just the result of bad bookkeeping; they're also the result of bad character. People whose decisions have resulted in the aggregate hurt of multiplied thousands of lives owe their misjudgment to their own rebellion against the law of God.

Wall Street is in trouble because some of its leaders have rejected the principles of truth in favor of immediate financial gratification. What would have happened if corporate America had learned, through the songs and Scriptures of childhood hours spent in a local church Sunday School, to love Jesus and His way of living?

Remember, Wall Street is not the "carrier" of free enterprise, where people are free to do right. But Sunday School is. Jesus said, "And you shall know the truth, and the truth shall make you free" (John 8:32). Sunday School is the place where people are introduced to Jesus who said, "Therefore if the Son makes you free, you shall be free indeed" (John 8:36). By the principles of truth, nations and kingdoms rise or fall. If that sounds a bit pre-

> *People don't naturally have character; it's something that's acquired over time and developed by training.*

sumptuous, then examine history! Christian education is simply that important!

Action Point: Your followers will not naturally develop the character they need to resist the pressures of the world. What can you do to help instill biblical character in them?

The Need for Christian Education

Christian education must be raised to its proper place in our churches. We are still following the teacher: "And so it was, when Jesus had ended these sayings, that the people were astonished at His teaching, for He taught them as one having authority, and not as the scribes" (Matt. 7:28-29). His teachings—affirmed by His lifestyle—made the difference to the thronged masses that gathered to hear His every word. The character of His apostles was formed by His teaching, and they went everywhere teaching what He taught them (see Matt. 28:20). Then the lives of those who heard the apostles were changed by the message, and they in turn changed the culture around them. Sunday School still provides the teaching and support to instill character in your congregation, and Sunday School will involve them as they reach out to the world with a message of discipleship. Notice how character is transferred.

Builds Self-Esteem

In a Sunday School, everybody counts. Each member is a valued part of the whole. That value begins with God who loves all, died for all and has a wonderful plan for all. When a person accepts God's plan for his or her life, he or she receives a sense of well-being. People who have self-worth are more likely to value others. That's what happens in Sunday School when both children and adults are recruited to serve others. They do it because they love and value others. They then become resistant to outside pressures.

Teaches Values

Many people lack values more than they lack character. Students may cheat, for instance, not because they are incapable of being honest, but because they've learned that cheating is acceptable. They have learned they can get away with it. They value getting ahead rather than their integrity. Sunday School teaches solid, biblical values such as honesty, integrity and faithfulness—which stay with believers in the playground, school, the workplace and life.

Provides Accountability

Members of a Sunday School class come to know each other well. If one member of the group lacks integrity at some point, others will know. And because Sunday School is a loving fellowship, members have the freedom to point out each other's shortcomings. The best thing about Sunday School fellowship is seeing yourself through the eyes of fellow class members. When students do that, they begin to see themselves through God's eyes.

Offers Support

A lone Christian in school or the workplace may tend to think, *It's me against the world*. It doesn't have to be that way. Sunday School class members offer encouragement and support to one another. A Sunday School class should give students the idea It's *us* against the world. Fellow class members provide the confidence everyone needs to make it through real-world choices.

▼

Are you looking for a way to influence the morality of your community? Sunday School will help. If a "little child will lead them," (Isa. 11:6) then that child must be pointed in the right direction, from his or her earliest years.

Are you looking for a way to involve the member of your church in vital ministry? Sunday School will help. Its opportunities for ministry are almost limitless. Its workers are waiting for a trumpet call, but in the meantime, they will assemble at the sound of a bugle.

The Marine Corps is not the only outfit looking for a few good men and women. The Church of Jesus Christ needs strong believers, good soldiers and people of character. Sunday School provides them.

Action Point: You lead an entire body of people called a church. How can you help each one develop more biblical character? Do you have a strong Sunday School in order to do this?

Chapter 19

SUNDAY SCHOOL ACTIVATES FRIENDSHIP EVANGELISM

Ruth and Cathy were having coffee at the realtor's office where they worked in sales. Cathy knew Ruth was older and wiser, so she took every opportunity to ask questions and learn.

"Our church is having a Friend Day," Ruth explained. "I'd like for you to come as my friend."

"Oh, no!" Cathy quickly resisted. "Your church is so big, and crowds scare me." Cathy explained that she had read in the newspapers that Ruth's church was called a "megachurch," and that intimidated her. Cathy also didn't like the pastor's well-known stand against abortion, so Cathy added, "I'm very open-minded, and I don't think your church is open-minded."

Ruth smiled and didn't try to calm Cathy's fears about her church, but she explained Friend Day. "My Sunday School class is small, about 20 people, and we'll have a special coffee time. Remember, we like coffee time."

They both laughed.

Ruth explained they had special activities on Friend Day. People who had special vehicles were displaying them on the lawn—antique cars, race cars and a humvee. There would be a special tent for children's refreshments, plus large inflatable jumping and sliding attractions. In the special receiving line, you would be able to meet the pastor and the city mayor, who was the special friend the pastor had invited for Friend Day. Then Ruth added, "You can ask him your questions yourself."

"I wouldn't do that," Cathy quickly responded. "But I'd love to be your friend and visit your church on Friend Day. I like to explore religions."

Cathy called herself an honest seeker. She had attended a Roman Catholic mass, a Bahai temple, a synagogue, and just last Saturday she had gone to a Seventh-Day Adventist church.

Cathy met Ruth in the church's parking lot on Friend Day. Cathy was immediately impressed when a friendly parking attendant greeted her before she got out of the car, opened the door for her and directed her to where she planned to meet Ruth. There were smiling greeters at every door to shake her hand, and the coffee time in the Sunday School class was as enjoyable as Ruth promised.

Instead of a lesson, the teacher shared his testimony, which was similar to Cathy's treks to different churches, searching for truth. Finally, the teacher explained, "I discovered I was searching for Jesus. I needed Him, not a church." The teacher quoted Jesus' words, "I am the way, the truth, and the life. No one comes to the Father except through Me" (John 14:6).

Cathy didn't stay for the worship service as she had promised. But on Monday night, two ladies from the church dropped by to bring Cathy a video of the church's praise worship service. One told Cathy, "This is contemporary music; you'll like it, and if you want, here's a cassette to play in your car."

The ladies met Mike, Cathy's husband, whom no one in the church had known about before then. When Cathy tried to ask some of her questions about religion, the ladies confessed they didn't know all the answers but would arrange for the teacher to visit Cathy and Mike. The following Sunday, Cathy returned to Sunday School, and the following Monday the Sunday School teacher visited her home to spend the evening answering Cathy's questions as best he could.

"Well, I don't have any more questions," Cathy said over her empty coffee cup.

"Does that mean you're ready to believe in Jesus Christ?"

"Yes," Cathy quietly bowed her head.

What Is Friendship Evangelism?

There are many techniques to reach people with the gospel, i.e., crusade evangelism, radio and TV evangelism, tract evangelism, etc. But *friendship evangelism* is as old as the Bible. When the Samaritan woman believed, she came back bringing the men of her village to hear Jesus' amazing news (see John 4:28-30). When Jesus cast the demons out of the man at Gadara, the man wanted to go travel with Jesus. But the Lord said, "Go home to your friends, and tell them what great things the Lord has done for you" (Mark 5:19). Cornelius the Roman army officer assembled his family and friends to hear the gospel (see Acts 10:24). The Philippian jailer asked what he had to do to be saved. He was told, "Believe on the Lord Jesus Christ, and you will be saved, you and your household" (Acts 16:31). When he believed, all of his family believed and were baptized with him.

Friendship evangelism has been called many things. First, *oikos evangelism* because the Greek word for household is *oikos*. Second, *web evangelism* because people reach others for Christ through the network, or web, of relationships. This type of evangelism is also known as F.R.A.N.gelism—each of the four letters in FRAN stands for Friends, Relatives, Associates and Neighbors. It is simply reaching people for Christ by networking through existing relationships.

Why Is It Effective?

The law of three hearings. Research has shown that most people don't make a decision to be converted or to join a church on their first visit. It usually takes people between two to four visits before they make a life-changing decision. They want their questions answered, they want to look at the life of those in the church, and they want to see if they truly get something out of the church service—if they experience the presence of God. The phrase "three hearings" means they make a decision to bond after they've attended at least three times to hear the message in a sermon or Sunday School lesson.

The law of seven touches. Statistics show visitors decide to join a church after they have had seven meaningful contacts with people from the church. Such contacts include letters, phone calls, home visits, appointments or visiting other informal church activities. Remember, a high-tech church must also be high-touch.

Who is most influential? A survey has been done in thousands of churches asking the question: Who is most responsible for influencing you to receive Jesus Christ? An informal survey in a local church concerning the influences that shape each person's decision to become a Christian produced the following results:

2% Had been influenced by religious advertisement
     (i.e., radio, TV, tracts or other nonpersonal form
     of evangelism)
6% Had been influenced by a pastoral staff member
6% Had been influenced by intentional or organized
     evangelism (i.e., visitation, state fair evangelism,
     street preaching, etc.)
86% Had been influenced by a friend or relative [1]

Action Point: How did most of the converts in your church come to Christ? How can you continue the use of these techniques in the future?

Can You Meet a Biblical Mandate?

Everyone is supposed to share the gospel with others. This is what Jesus intended when He said, "You shall be witnesses to Me" (see Acts 1:8). A witness—like one on a court witness stand—simply tells others what he has experienced; i.e., what he saw and heard and what part, if any, he had in the event. So too your church members should be sharing with friends and family how Jesus Christ changed their lives.

The members of the Early Church went all over Jerusalem telling everyone what had happened to them: "For we cannot but speak the things which we have seen and heard" (Acts 4:20).

Most evangelical pastors exhort their congregation to be good witnesses, to share the gospel with their friends or to be active in soul winning. This encouragement is done from the pulpit. But again, research reveals that most Christians are more effective in evangelism when they have a program that motivates them to reach out and a place—a Sunday School class—to which the new convert can be invited to attend.

When prospects join a church, they don't usually identify with the large congregational meeting called a worship service.

New members usually bond with a primary group; e.g., a choir, Sunday School class or service committee, and proudly inform others "I'm an usher" or "I belong to the women's circle at my church." Is a Sunday School class the primary group for many at your church?

Sunday School is the most important instrument your church will ever have when it comes to friendship evangelism. Don't neglect to use it! Let those who have made a decision for Christ learn to witness to Christ—in Sunday School.

Action Point: How can you move your members from being just church members to become active witnesses for Christ?

DON'T GIVE UP ON SUNDAY SCHOOL

Many pastors have given up on Sunday School. Why? Have they given up because Sunday School is so traditional and loaded down with baggage from a past era? If so, strip away the old and polish up the original purpose. Sunday School is the church at work teaching the Bible.

Some have given up on Sunday School to run after small home-group classes called cells. Some pastors have given up on Sunday School, substituting Wednesday-night Bible institutes. And although the other programs of Bible teaching are good, and church cells have their place and purpose, most people expect to attend a church on Sunday morning. And they expect it to have a place to teach them the Bible.

What will happen if we give up on Sunday School? If pastors—our church leaders—give up, will not our workers also give up?

If our Sunday School workers give up on Sunday School, what will happen to those who attend? Won't they also give up?

If pastors give up on Sunday School, it will eventually die without leadership.

What will happen to the American church that gives up on Sunday School? It will not have a place of systematic Bible teaching.

If the American church gives up on Sunday School, it will become as anemic as the Church in England and Europe. These churches—while still alive—do not have the influence on their society that the American church does on its society.

While the American church is not perfect, and the American church does not have the influence on society it once had, it still has life. The atheists and secular humanists still fight the influence of the American church in Congress, state legislatures, courts, schoolhouses and media. They are angry at the church's influence and want to snuff out the church's voice and influence.

Can they do it? Yes: If Sunday School dies, then our people won't know the Bible! The Church can't influence society with just preaching and worship. To influence society, it will take Christians who know the Bible and can apply it to life. It will take involved Christians who are using their spiritual gifts in service to their church and their community. And where will the Christians come from who have biblical knowledge and are trained to serve God? The Sunday School (and you can use this book as a starting-point tool).

If you give up on Sunday School, you have given up on one of the greatest tools to positively influence lives, to positively influence your church and to positively influence your nation. Sunday School carries out the command of Jesus, "Teaching them to observe all things that I have commanded" (Matt. 28:20). Never give up!

Endnotes

Chapter 3

1. Tim LaHaye, *The Battle of the Mind* (Grand Rapids, MI: Fleming H. Revell, 1980).

Chapter 6

1. Dennis Williams and Kenneth O. Gangel, *Volunteers for Today's Church: How to Recruit and Retain Workers* (Grand Rapids, MI: Baker Books, 1993), p. 9.

Chapter 7

1. Michael J. Anthony, ed., *Foundations of Ministry, An Introduction to Christian Education for a New Generation* (Wheaton, IL: Victor Books, 1992), p. 168.

Chapter 8

1. Steve Rabey, *In Search of Authentic Faith: How Emerging Generations Are Transforming the Church* (Colorado Springs, CO: Waterbrook Press, 2001), p. 148.
2. Dennis Williams and Kenneth O. Gangel, *Volunteers for Today's Church: How to Recruit and Retain Workers* (Grand Rapids, MI: Baker Books, 1993), p. 23.

Chapter 9

1. Denny Gunderson, *The Leadership Paradox: A Challenge to Servant Leadership in a Power Hungry World* (Seattle, WA: Youth With a Mission Publishing, 1997), p. 140.

Chapter 10

1. Talmadge Johnson and Stan Toler, *Rediscovering the Sunday School* (Kansas City, MO: Beacon Hill Press of Kansas City, 2000), p. 29.

Chapter 11

1. Dennis H. Dirks, "Foundations of Human Development," in *Foundations of Ministry, An Introduction to Christian Education for a New Generation,* ed. Michael J. Anthony (Wheaton, IL: Victor Books, 1992), p. 71.

Chapter 12

1. Steve Rabey, *In Search of Authentic Faith: How Emerging Generations Are Transforming the Church* (Colorado Springs, CO: Waterbrook Press, 2001), p. 77.

Chapter 13

1. Dennis E. Williams and Kenneth O. Gangel, *Volunteers for Today's Church: How to Recruit and Retain Workers* (Grand Rapids, MI: Baker Books, 1993), p. 142.

Chapter 17

1. Talmadge Johnson and Stan Toler, *Rediscovering the Sunday School* (Kansas City, MO: Beacon Hill Press of Kansas City, 2000), pp. 74-75.

Chapter 19

1. This informal survey was conducted by Elmer Towns between 1987 and 2002. The statistics quoted here are the results of his questioning and are used to illustrate the principle of Friendship Evangelism.

Also from Elmer L. Towns

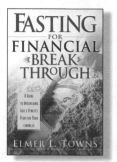

Fasting for Financial Breakthrough
A Guide to Uncovering God's Perfect Plan for Your Finances
Elmer L. Towns
Trade Paper
ISBN 08307.29631

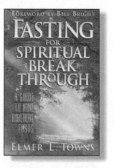

Fasting for Spiritual Breakthrough
A Guide to Nine Biblical Fasts
Elmer L. Towns
Trade Paper
ISBN 08307.18397
Study Guide
ISBN 08307.18478

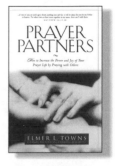

Prayer Partners
How to Increase the Power and Joy of Your Prayer Life by Praying with Others
Elmer L. Towns
Trade Paper
ISBN 08307.29348

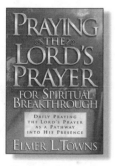

Praying the Lord's Prayer for Spiritual Breakthrough
Praying the Lord's Prayer Daily As a Pathway into His Presence
Elmer L. Towns
Paperback
ISBN 08307.20421
Video Study Package
UPC 607135.002901

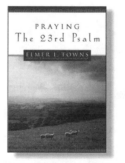

Praying the 23rd Psalm
"The Lord is my Shepherd; I shall not want"
Elmer L. Towns
Paperback
ISBN 08307.27760

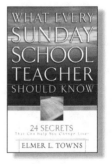

What Every Sunday School Teacher Should Know
24 Secrets that Can Help You Change Lives
Elmer L. Towns
Mass
ISBN 08307.28740
Video
UPC 607135.006091

Regal
God's Word for Your World™

Available at your local Christian bookstore.
www.regalbooks.com

Also from Stan Toler

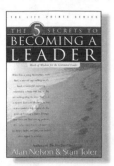

The Five Secrets to Becoming a Leader
Words of Wisdom for the Untrained Leader
Alan Nelson and *Stan Toler*
Mass
ISBN 08307.29151

The Five-Star Church
Serving God and His People with Excellence
Stan Toler and *Alan Nelson*
Paperback
ISBN 08307.23501

Leading Your Sunday School into the 21st Century
Elmer L. Towns and *Stan Toler*
Video
UPC 607135.002581

Evangelism and Church Growth Reference Library CD-ROM
21 Complete Books on One CD-ROM
Various Authors
CD-ROM, Windows
ISBN 08307.25202

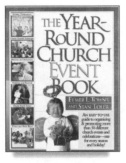

The Year-Round Church Event Book
A Step-by-Step Guide to Planning and Promoting Successful Events
Elmer L. Towns and *Stan Toler*
Manual, reproducible
ISBN 08307.20405

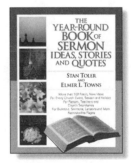

The Year-Round Book of Sermon Ideas, Stories and Quotes
Ready-to-Use Stories, Quotes and Sermon Helps for Any Event
Stan Toler and *Elmer L. Towns*
Manual, reproducible
ISBN 08307.25725

Regal
God's Word for Your World™

Available at your local Christian bookstore.
www.regalbooks.com